Opting For The Poor

Brazilian Catholicism in Transition

Madeleine Adriance

Sheed & Ward

Sheed and Ward™ is a service of National Catholic Reporter Publish-
ing, Inc.

Library of Congress Catalog Card Number: 85-63108

ISBN: 0-934134-75-8

Published by:

Sheed and Ward
115 E. Armour Blvd. P.O. Box 281
Kansas City, MO 64141-0281

To order, call: (800) 821-7926

Contents

Foreword

Rarely does one encounter an author who succeeds in balancing a clear value commitment with the relentless pursuit of the truth. Madeleine Adriance has attained this balance in her study of the preferential option for the poor as it emerged within Brazilian Catholicism. A North American who understands the Latin American spirit, she combines scientific sociological inquiry with a genuine sensitivity to the viewpoint of people who have been experiencing the process of change in the Church. She guides the reader through an exploration of political and economic changes that presented new challenges for the Church's pastoral mission, the formation of religious structures that helped to produce innovations to respond to those challenges, the subsequent military repression that led to the persecution of activists both inside and outside the Church, and, finally, the establishment of the option for the poor as an integral part of Catholic belief that is evident in the documents of the National Conference of the Brazilian Bishops and the Latin American Bishops Conference.

I first met Madeleine Adriance during a course at Boston College in 1982, when she came to ask me about my perceptions of the basic ecclesial communities. At that time I was struck by her deep interest in and intuitive grasp of Third World realities. I urged her to come to Brazil to do further research, which she eventually was able to do. In the four months that she was here, she very quickly gained an unusual degree of insight about the land, its people, and their faith. Since she is not the sort of "radical" intellectual who thinks that history is made inside of one's own head, she sought to learn about the social origins of the option for the poor by going to live among poor people in a rural village for a month, and attempting in her own way to share as much as she could of the way of life of the people there, that she even began to ask bishops and other formally educated people about their interpretations of the situation. Perhaps it was because she began by trying to learn from the people themselves that she so quickly developed an understanding of the Brazilian Catholic experience.

Another consequence of the author's efforts to learn from Brazilians of all social backgrounds is the human quality of her narrative. People's perceptions of their own reality emerge in the numerous quotes from interviews that appear throughout the book. Peasants and archbishops, religious sisters and union organizers all speak in these pages. At the same time, this subjective element is balanced by a careful institutional analysis that demonstrates the internal dynamics of the Church both at the national and at the world level.

At a time when there is a continuing controversy over the question of whether Christians can utilize Marxian social analysis without compromising their Christianity, Adriance demonstrates a serene integration of these two perspectives. Never abandoning her appreciation of religion both as a personally meaningful system of faith and as a factor in social transformations, she presents a dialectical explanation of the mutual influence of changes that occur in the political-economic and religious spheres. Her thorough understanding of the real meaning of class conflict and of structural-historical processes is used in order to cast light on the question of how religion can be liberating in every sense of the word. To persons who feel unable to accept the idea that a Christian may use Marxism as a tool of intellectual analysis, I would say, look at this book. The author's motivation is religious, her sociological framework clearly draws on the insights of Marx and Gramsci, and neither Christianity nor Marxism appears to suffer from the association.

But the fruits of this synthesis go far beyond the mere absence of harm. What we have here is an important documentation — a record of the development of the preferential option for the poor that shows its genesis and its consequences in both the Church and the larger society. By gathering this valuable information, Madeleine Adriance has provided for North Americans a means of understanding what is happening in Latin America today, in relation to the peoples' struggles for liberation, the transformations in the Church, and the points of intersection between these two processes. This contribution is of both present relevance and long-range significance.

Paulo Freire
Catholic University of São Paulo

PREFACE

This book began as a study of the relationship between religion and social change in Brazil. What emerged, however, was the story of a Church that has been living through a great deal of pain and growth. In the telling of this story, I have tried to include the points of view of the people who have been experiencing it and have also tried, in translating their statements made in Portuguese, to stay as close as possible to what they actually said.

I claim no freedom from bias. As a committed Christian and humanistic sociologist, I am deeply concerned about the political-economic structures that perpetuate oppression, and I am searching for ways to work toward changing those structures. At the same time, this book is not a polemical work. The research on which it is based challenged some of my own cherished assumptions — including the belief that there is a new Catholic Church in Brazil which is emerging entirely from the grassroots and in which poor people always have a voice — and it forced me to distinguish empirical observation from wishful thinking.

In the process of writing, I have been filled with a deep sense of gratitude to the incredible number of people who made my research possible. Because of the sensitive political situation in Brazil, several persons asked that their names not be mentioned. Regarding others, I will leave unmentioned most of those presently in Brazil, except for some who would not likely be harmed, either because of their prominent positions or because they have already survived so much public controversy that any association with my research would be insignificant by comparison.

I would like to express my very deep appreciation to Sally Cassidy and Paule Verdet, whose encouragement, support and friendship went far above and beyond the duty of academic advisors and without whose help this book could not have been written; Sister Marie Augusta Neal, my first sociology professor, who gave me an early enthusiasm for the subject, a great deal of encouragement with my work over the years and more recent help in the form of contacts in Brazil and a letter of introduction that opened many Church doors; Otto Maduro, Alicja Iwanska, Denis Goulet, John Eagleson and Reverend Victor Schymeinsky, who were also very helpful in providing contacts with persons in Brazil; and Ellen Hill, who offered helpful criticisms of an earlier draft of the manuscript.

Another group of people deserving of great thanks are those in the United States who consented to be interviewed about their experiences in Brazil — Loretta Slover, Therese Drummond; Sisters Gertrude Baron and Ellen Dabreio; Fathers Alexander Weiss, Thomas Jones, John Walsh, John Maynard and Cornelius Lynch.

Those in Brazil whom I would like to thank for interviews, advice and/or further contacts are Marina Bandeira, Lourdes Santos, Florence Anderson, Dagmar Zibas, Luiza Fernandes, Francisco Whitaker, Paulo Freire, Francisco Julião, Paulo Crespo, Frei G.S. Gorgulho, Frei Romeo Dale, Monseignor Expedito Sobral de Medeiros, Dom António Costa, Dom José Lamartine Soares, Dom Luiz Fernandes, Dom Marcelo Cavalheira, Dom Hélder Câmara and Dom Paulo Evaristo Arns. Special thanks go to Father Clodovis Boff and to Professors Sebastião Vila Nova and Luiz Eduardo Wanderley for academic advice that drew on both their personal experiences and their sociological insights.

It has been difficult to determine which persons may be thanked by name and which ones should remain anonymous.

Preface

I only hope that I have neither offended anyone by exclusion nor harmed anyone by inclusion. To so many people who gave me friendship, time, information, contacts and very generous hospitality — to all of you who specifically asked me not to mention your names, or whose permission to mention them I forgot to ask — I can only say *muito obrigada*.

That we are living in a time of change is evident in my final and greatest acknowledgment. It has been a tradition for male authors to thank their wives for being supportive during long hours of research and writing. I owe a great debt of gratitude to my husband, Frank Adriance, for being mother and father to our children during the four months I was in Brazil, and to our children, Lisa and David, for being understanding about my absence, for respecting the closed door of my study and, most of all, for greeting me with lots of hugs and kisses when the door opens. This book is lovingly dedicated to Frank, David and Lisa.

1
EXPLORATIONS

Where did it begin? Was it in São Paulo, that swelling, cosmopolitan, stimulating and alienating industrial giant in the south of Brazil? Or was it in São Paulo do Potengí, a quiet, simple, remote rural town in a far corner of the drought-ridden Brazilian northeast?

And *when* did it begin? When did the Roman Catholic Church change its definition of charity from almsgiving to the struggle for social justice? When did the Latin American Catholic community and institution begin its journey toward a new position that would involve the nurturing of grassroots movements for social change, as well as conflict with political authorities — a position that has come to be known as "the preferential option for the poor"? Was it in 1968, at the historic meeting of the bishops in Medellín, Columbia? Was it a few years earlier, in Rome at the Second Vatican Council? Or were some sectors of the Church really far ahead of the rest of the Christian world in preparing the foundation for a liberation theology[1] that would go beyond previous Catholic and Protestant social teachings?

Brazil has been of key importance[2] in this process of religious change, which began in the 1950's and the early 1960's. Brazil was the first country in which the preferential option for the poor began to be articulated in official statements by the bishops, as well as one in which new religious and political activity at the grassroots, in the form of the basic ecclesial communities (CEBs), first became visible. It was important as a location of religious innovations that would provide vehicles for further changes. Most notably, it was the first country in which a national conference of bishops was established, as well as one of the first in which the Catholic Action movement[3] was reorganized from the traditional Italian version to the French version, which placed a greater emphasis on lay leadership and social action.

In addition to these religious factors, Brazil has also provided a prototype for political-economic changes in Latin-America — beginning with increasingly rapid industrialization and urbanization as early as the 1930's, an attempt at constitutional democracy between 1945 and 1964, the increasing involvement of foreign corporations in its economy and finally, after 1964, a new kind of military regime — one characterized not only by the violent repression traditionally utilized by dictatorships, but also by sophisticated scientific principles of long-range political planning, supported by financial and technical assistance from the United States. For all these reasons, it would seem that to trace the development of the preferential option for the poor in Brazilian Catholicism would provide a foundation for understanding related religious phenomena in other parts of Latin America and of the Third World, such as the political activism of nuns and priests in Central America and the courageous human rights positions taken by bishops in the Phillippines.

The option for the poor is manifested at different levels within the Church. Among intellectuals it takes the form of liberation theology — that is, the articulation of the belief that people's eternal salvation is inseparable from their involvement in the struggle toward the radical transformation of social structures that perpetuate poverty and repression. Although the writings of liberation theologians [4] indicate the Biblical roots of their beliefs, it is also clear that their emphasis on the prophetic[5] cry for justice has developed in interaction with the Latin American social context.

On the level of Church policy-making, the option for the poor is reflected in the official statements of national bishops' conferences (such as the National Conference of the Brazilian Bishops, or CNBB), and in the documents resulting from the meetings of the Latin American Bishops Conference (CELAM) at Medellín and at Puebla.[6] In addition to statements on human rights, these documents include specific recommendations about economic development and the social empowerment of peasants, factory workers and indigenous peoples.

The most concrete level of the implementation of the Church's option for the poor is that of the basic ecclesial communities (CEBs) — those small grassroots groups of people who come together for prayer, Scriptural reflection and social action — of which there are estimated to be as many as one hundred thousand in Brazil alone. For it is there that the religious and political implications of the preferential option for the poor come to life. It is through the CEBs that poor people are encouraged to organize religious activities with the assistance of lay leaders, suggesting some kind of change in the traditional domination of Catholic congregations by the clergy. And this experience which CEB members have of religious participation is often transferred to an increase in their political participation as well. For example, many observers of the Brazilian political scene believe that the resurgence of grassroots movements in Brazil in the late 1970's and the popular demands for a return to a democratic form of government in the early-to-middle 1980's were strongly influenced by people who were active in the basic communities.

Along with the questions of when and where the preferential

option for the poor began to develop, there is also the question of how. What was it that made the Church change? There is a paradox in social and religious change insofar as radical transformations are sometimes rooted in actions initially taken for conservative reasons. To be more specific, the preferential option for the poor, which, as will be shown later, may present serious challenges to both religious and political structures of power, began with adaptations made by clergy who were concerned about the threat to the Church's influence that was presented in the 1950's by socialism and evangelical Protestantism. However, once these adaptations became institutionalized (that is, made a permanent feature of the Church's official position), the option for the poor became a religious end in itself, independent of any perceived external pressure. This institutionalization of the new ecclesial position was particularly salient in Brazil, where the military coup removed the "Communist threat." In the changed political-economic context of an authoritarian regime, the option for the poor led the Church to become a vehicle for land struggles, organized labor and other popular movements. Thus the position of the Catholic Church vis-à-vis the political sphere was redefined.

In order to understand how the development of the preferential option for the poor could begin with attempts toward ecclesial self-preservation, one must consider the religious goal of Christianity and the specific means by which the Brazilian Catholic Church had traditionally attempted to meet that goal. Christianity is a salvation religion. In general terms, this means that its goal is to reach out to people for the purpose of saving their immortal souls. Some Christian sects strive toward that goal through inspirational crusades aimed at the awakening of individual persons' commitment to Jesus as their personal savior. The Roman Catholic Church, by contrast, has traditionally been oriented toward the overall influencing of society, for the purpose of creating a social climate that encouraged people to observe Catholic ethics and ritual practices. In Latin America, until very recently, bishops generally believed that the best means of carrying out their mission of salvation was to reach out to the elite classes and to assume that the masses would follow — an approach particularly well-suited to a continent with a historical shortage of clergy. Consequently, priests and bishops formed alliances with large landowners, as well as with political and military leaders, and encouraged the formation of Catholic lay organizations (such as Opus Dei, general Catholic Action, the Legion of Mary and various brotherhoods) among the upper classes. In addition to encouraging piety among wealthy people, the clergy relied upon them to organize and contribute financial support to the Church's various charities. Religious sisters were usually assigned to teach in elite private schools, in the belief that they would thus inculcate Christian values in the future leaders of society. Christian Democratic parties were similarly encouraged as a means of influencing society through its leaders.

By the 1950's, however, it was becoming evident that the masses were not always going along with the elites, and that the majority of Latin Americans had no particular organizational loyalty toward the Catholic Church. At first, the response of the hierarchy to this new situation was to encourage pastoral innovations and social reform projects for the purpose of restoring the Church's influence over society.[7] However, the institutionalization of these measures would eventually result in some real changes in the Church's position in relation to the poor and in a new social role for religion.

This type of explanation is sometimes disturbing to people with religious convictions because, at first glance, it appears to negate the dimension of faith. To understand how this is not necessarily the case, it is important to distinguish between religious and sociological — or structural — explanations of religious change. While bishops may explain Church policy in terms of their mission of salvation, social scientists may interpret the very same policy as functioning to preserve the Church's influence. Although these two interpretations may appear to be antagonistic, they actually represent related dimensions of religion. In other words, religion is both a social institution, with a tendency toward self-preservation, and a system of personal meaning centered on faith.

In order to study the origins of religious change, it is necessary to examine both structural-institutional priorities and the faith-inspired viewpoint of the religious believer. Throughout this book, the effort is made to present both dimensions, the former through a sociological analysis of historical events and the latter through excerpts from Church documents and from interviews with persons who have actually experienced the changing Brazilian Catholic Church. The interviews were part of a research project I conducted in Brazil, which also involved the study of Church documents, some lived experience with a rural basic ecclesial community and observations of seven other CEBs and of larger gatherings of CEB representatives in several different regions of the country. The sixty-four people whom I interviewed included lay members of basic communities, religious sisters, seminarians, priests, bishops and persons who had been involved in specific religious or political movements. Most of them were Brazilian, although a few were foreign missionaries (mostly from the United States). I have quoted these people throughout most of my account, in the hope of allowing them to tell their own story. That story is told in the context of a particular society during a particular time period, a context characterized by a dynamic interaction between different elements — that is, between the Church and the larger society as well as between the changing positions of bishops and the activism of people at the grassroots. A grasp of these dynamic relationships is very helpful in understanding the development of the Church's present political and pastoral direction. To communicate a sense of this process, the chapters which follow are presented in an alternating pattern, with one chapter tracing conflicts or changes in the Brazilian political-economic context and the next one indicating related developments within the Catholic Church. This alternating pattern should convey some idea of the subtle interplay between religion and the social structure, as well as tell the story of the preferential option for the poor.

NOTES

[1]Liberation theology is defined on page 2

[2]Chile was also of key importance. It would be imposssible to credit either Brazil or Chile as having been the only milieu for the emergence of the preferential option for the poor. With regard to the various elements described in this paragraph and in the next, Brazil was the first for some, while Chile was the first for others. It may be important to note that Dom Manuel Larraín, who was the bishop of Talca, Chile, until his death in the late 1960's, was in close communication wiht Dom Hélder Câmara, who was an auxiliary bishop in Rio de Janeiro in the 1950's and who became archbishop of Olinda and Recife in 1964. Both bishops were very influential in organizing the Second General Conference of the Latin American Bishops in Medellín, Colombia, which is viewed as a turning point in the position of the Catholic Church.

[3]Catholic Action, along with its reorganization from the Italian to the French model, is described in Chapter Three.

[4]See Gustavo Gutierrez, *A Theology of Liberation* (Maryknoll, N.Y.: Orbis Books, 1973); José Porfirio Miranda, *Marx and the Bible: A Critique of the Philosophy of Oppression* (Maryknoll, N.Y.: Orbis Books, 1974); Leonardo Boff, *Jesus Christ Liberator: A Critical Christology for our Time* (Maryknoll, N.Y.: Orbis Books, 1978); Alejandro Cussianovich, *Religious Life and the Poor* (Maryknoll, N.Y.: Orbis Books, 1979).

[5]"Prophetic" in this context refers to the socially critical positions that were taken by some of the Biblical prophets.

[6]The Third General Conference of the Latin American Bishops took place in Puebla, Mexico, in 1979. It went beyond the preferential option for the poor

expressed at the Second General Conference in Medellín, Colombia, in 1968, insofar as the bishops at Puebla approved documents that took a stronger and more explicit position on human rights.

[7]See Ivan Vallier, *Catholicism, Social Control, and Modernization in Latin America* (Englewood Cliffs, N.J.: Prentice-Hall, 1970) and Thomas C. Bruneau, *The Political Transformation of the Brazilian Catholic Church* (London: Cambridge University Press, 1974).

2
THE BRAZILIAN POLITICAL-ECONOMIC CONTEXT FROM 1930 TO 1950

1930 is often considered to have been a turning point for Brazil. It was the year of the coup d'état that brought Getúlio Vargas to power, and it was also the year that marked the beginning of the economic consequences of the Great Depression.

Prior to 1930, Brazil had had an import-export economy based mainly on the production of coffee in the south and sugar in the northeast, and on a relationship of economic dependency with England (which would later be replaced by a similar relationship with the United States). Coffee and sugar were exported, and industrial products, as well as some foods, were imported. Brazil was unusual among neo-colonial[1] countries, however, in that almost all of the coffee-producing land remained in the hands of Brazilians. The favorable position of these plantation owners in relation to the expanding world market for coffee would result in their accumulation of large profits. Some of the coffee growers invested their profits in new manufacturing enterprises, thus forming the basis for the beginnings of domestic industry.[2]

With the Great Depression, the price of coffee on the world market fell drastically. The international economic crisis also resulted in the reduction of the import market, creating a scarcity of manufactured goods. So there was a double incentive to invest increasing amounts of coffee money into new local factories, which would have consequences for the way of life of large numbers of people. The expanding industries lured hundreds of thousands of impoverished peasants off the land and into the factories, and, between 1920 and 1940, the number of industrial workers in Brazil almost tripled.

This beginning of a gradual shift in the economic base of Brazil from a semi-feudal agricultural economy to manufacturing would have an effect on government policy. Vargas realized that, in order to stay in power, he would have to meet the demands both of the large landowners and of the new industrial entrepreneurs. His sense of how to maintain this balance would be reflected in specific government measures to satisfy these different vested interests, as will be shown below.

In building his power base, Vargas was also aware of the importance of establishing an alliance with the Catholic Church, which his political predecessors had tended to neglect. The liberal, even anti-clerical ideology of most of the previous presidents of Brazil had led them to downplay Church-state relations. Many of the bishops, on the other hand, still lived in nostalgia for colonial times, when the Church had enjoyed a relatively favorable position as the state religion and when the wishes of the hierarchy were often reflected in government policy. Consequently, in 1930, Dom Sebastião Leme de Silveira Cintra, the Cardinal-Archbishop of Rio de Janeiro, was quite willing to play an active role in helping Vargas to come to power.[3] This favor would not be forgotten by the dictator. Although his new constitution officially maintained the separation of Church and state, it also contained certain provisions that favored the position of the Church — such as religious instruction in the public schools, the prohibition of divorce, the provision of government and military chaplaincies and financial assistance to Catholic schools and to the Church as a whole.

It is important to note that this new situation would reinforce the attitude held by the bishops and by some government leaders that for the Church to have a strong influence over Brazilian society through the government was a normal and desirable state of affairs. This attitude would persist within the government for over thirty years, and within the Church for a few years longer. It would be reflected in actions taken by both religious and political officials to cope with the social problems that would arise as a result of changes in the economic context that were already beginning to occur at the very same time that the Church-state alliance was being established.

Throughout the 1930's, the scarcity of manufactured imports continued to stimulate growth in the domestic manufacture of products for local consumption. Furthermore, the political structure set up by Vargas provided for the government's management of economic stimulants — such as taxes, wages, import quotas and the state control of labor unions — all of which were favorable to the interests of the wealthy new industrialists. The entry in 1942 of Brazil into World War II increased the need for manufactured products related to war, and allowed for the justification of even more government intervention in the economy. So under the dictatorship that lasted until 1945, the urban industrial elite continued to prosper.

Vargas also managed to preserve the loyalty of the rural landowning elite by means of measures to mitigate the effects of the Depression on their prosperity. These measures included the government purchase of coffee surpluses, the regulation of prices and the prevention of political participation by agricultural laborers. He also pleased the sugar cane growers in the northeast region. In the early 1930's, sugar plantation owners had been exerting pressure for measures to protect their profits. In 1934, the government established quotas of minimum production and, through the regulation of imports, reserved the national market for sugar produced in Brazil. In 1936, the Statute of Cane Production established a guarantee for the plantation owners that at least forty percent of their harvest would be processed by the sugar mills. These measures would have two consequences:

(1) They would guarantee both the prosperity of the cane producers and their political loyalty to Vargas;

(2) They would establish the foundation for profound changes in the mode of agricultural production, and these changes would have severely negative consequences for the peasants.

Until the late 1930's, the agricultural system in the cane-producing northeast region had been virtually feudal. Each peasant family residing on a plantation had access to a plot of land for subsistence farming. In return, they were obliged to work two or three days each week for the plantation owner (in his cane fields, for example) at a rate of pay that was well below that of the non-resident wage-laborer. In addition, there were also tenant farmers who paid for the rental of plots of land, generally the most distant ones on the plantation, as well as having to contribute unpaid labor for a certain number of days each year. This traditional system of land use permitted a certain flexibility for the large landowners. For example, whenever there was a crisis in sugar prices, they would convert to subsistence farming (rice, beans, corn and manioc) and use the work obligations of the peasants and tenant farmers to facilitate the switch. However, the new government supports for the cane growers removed the need for this flexibility and supplied an incentive for the plantation owners to convert as much land as possible to permanent cane production. In this process, the peasants and the tenant farmers appeared to stand in the way of higher profits.

The consequence of this situation was the capitalization of agriculture — that is, the massive conversion of rural production to the capitalist model. In large numbers, peasants were evicted from their homes and were replaced by wage laborers, who lived apart from the work place — usually in shacks along the roadside or in a shanty town on the periphery of a city, if one was nearby. (Unlike the peasants, rural wage laborers had no access to any land on which they could grow their own food, and their meager incomes could suddenly be lost because of the hiring-firing cycles of capitalist production.) Landless peasants either became wage workers on other plantations or migrated to cities and became wage workers in the new industries, particularly in São Paulo. With the great demand for cheap industrial labor, bus companies from the south installed a network of ticket agencies throughout the rural northeast, thus accelerating the exodus to the industrial areas and the rapid urbanization of Brazil.

In this process of urbanization, there were combinations of migration patterns. In some cases, cane workers dissatisfied with the inhumane conditions of the new agricultural system joined the swell of dispossessed peasants on the urban periphery. In many instances, migrants moved first to provincial capitals in the northeast and, unable to find adequate employment there, would later move on to the industrializing south. There was also a two-way pattern that involved one or more members of a household, usually men of various ages and the younger, unmarried women. These would go to the south for periods of time to look for work, hoping to send money to the rest of the family remaining in the northeast, and would return home at intervals of varying regularity.

These migrations would result in a gradual shift of millions of people from the semi-feudal northeast region to the urban-industrial center-south. They would also result in the rapid growth of *favelas* (squatter slums) around the cities of Rio de

Janeiro and São Paulo, as the supply of cheap housing fell far
below the demand.

   This combination of factors — industrialization, urbanization
and the capitalization of agricultural production — all contributed to changes in the way of life of the people of the poorer
classes and, consequently, in their consciousness. Until that
time, they had viewed the social world in which they lived and
the conditions under which they had to work as though they
were created by God and therefore unchangeable. However,
the speed at which their lives were changing caused them to
lose some of their fatalism. As the social structure gradually
became demystified, there began to develop a potential for the
relations existing between the large landowners and the rural
poor to lose their appearance of being divinely ordained. That
appearance had already been disrupted by those landowners
who had thrown the peasants off the land. The existing order
was further demystified by the migrants who periodically returned to the northeast. They had experienced a whole new
way of life in the industrial south, where there was already a
modernized society that was very different from the traditions
of the northeast, and they shared their new awareness with
their fellow villagers. The consequent demystification of the
social structure produced a consciousness, among some of the
peasants, of the unnecessary nature of their poverty. This new
consciousness would lead them to be receptive to the efforts of
rural community organizers.

   The effects of these rapid social changes would also be felt
within the Church. The sudden growth in urban populations,
both in the center-south and in the northeast, led to an increased demand on the traditional religious vehicles of charity,
leading some clergy and social workers to begin to question the
whole assistentialist[4] approach to social problems. In the archdiocese of Natal, in the northeast state of Rio Grande do
Norte, for example, this approach was being modified as early

as the 1940's (as will be shown in Chapter Three).

In addition, the loss of the traditional rural community by the urban migrants resulted in the weakening of the influence of Catholicism over this rapidly increasing sector of the population — an influence that had been based on folk religion rooted in village customs, rather than on close pastoral ties between clergy and laity. After World War II, there was a sudden increase in Protestantism in Brazil. The expulsion of missionaries from China had led to the redirection of Evangelical Christians to Latin America, backed by generous financing from churches in the United States. The appeal of the small, close-knit Protestant congregations was greatest in the urban areas, among people with weakened community ties.

Religious syncretism — which is the combining of beliefs and rituals from more than one tradition, such as folk Catholicism, spiritism[5] and African and Native American religions — had always been an integral part of life in the rural areas. Nevertheless, it had not been very visible in those places to most of the Church leaders, who spent little or no time in remote villages. With the mass migrations to the cities, however, the number of cultic centers and retail establishments selling cultic materials suddenly increased to the point of becoming very visible. Consequently, it appeared to the hierarchy that adherence to the syncretist cults was on the increase, and a great deal of pastoral concern was expressed on this matter. Such a concern was clearly stated in a letter written by the Belgian priest-sociologist François Houtart from São Paulo to friends in Chicago, dated July 30, 1954:

> In Rio there are already more than six hundred spiritist temples officially registered. In São Paulo there are one hundred eighty . . . The bishops are very worried about this situation, since it affects

mostly Catholics . . . Because of the shortage of priests, there is no one to teach the people to do better.

(translation from French)

Finally, in the cane-producing regions, abuses associated with the new system of agricultural production resulted in such inhumane living and working conditions that they began to come to the attention of some of the clergy. The latter became concern about doing something to help the rural workers.

In the changing political-economic context, Church leaders were finding that their traditional pastoral assumptions were no longer useful for carrying out the mission of salvation. For example, the clergy were discovering that they could not take for granted the religiosity and loyalty of the masses of people. Furthermore, those who were genuinely concerned about the deteriorating conditions of the poor began to experience a challenge to their assumptions about the charitableness of the landowners (the traditional financers of Church-based programs of social assistance). It would be in the northeast region, where the social problems arising from the transformations in the political-economic context between 1930 and 1950 were most acute, that there would emerge the first signs of change in the Brazilian Catholic Church.

NOTES

[1]Under the traditional colonialism, the colony usually supplied raw materials to the dominant country, which considered the colony to be its possession, usually by reason of military conquest. Neo-colonialism is a bit more subtle. The dominant country is not officially considered to be the owner of the dependent country, but rather exercises control by reason of a more highly developed economy and technology. In additon to raw materials, the dependent country provides agricultural and industrial labor at a wage rate far below that which

prevails in the dominant country (as a result of the earlier development of labor unions in the latter), providing the incentive for investors from the dominant country to base much of their production in the dependent country. Because these foreign investors (in the present day, multinational corporations) retain control of the means of production, they determine what will be produced — such as cash crops and industrial products for export, rather than goods and food for local consumption. This orientation to foreign markets helps to intensify the relationship of dependency. The dominated country depends on the dominant country both as a market for the products and as a source of basic needs (including food). Furthermore, for most neo-colonial dependent countries, the ownership of the means of production by foreign interests results in a draining of wealth (1) through the removal of raw materials and (2) through the very low ratio of wages paid in relation to the profits extracted. This process of neo-colonial take-over is facilitated by the cooptation of the local elites into the new economic system and by political corruption in the dependent country. This whole package is usually presented as "development." This is the pattern characteristic of most "underdeveloped" countries, including contemporary Brazil. This was not the case, however, before the 1950's. Although Brazil partially followed the neo-colonial model, insofar as it was dependent on foreign countries for markets for its cash crops (coffee, sugar, cotton and tobacco) and for the importation of food and industrial products that it was not producing (because of this priority on exports), much of the land, including the valuable coffee lands in the south, remained in the ownership of wealthy Brazilians, and not of foreigners. It was coffee money that would form the basis for the development of Brazilian-owned industry in São Paulo.

[2]Unlike many of the following chapters, this one was not based mainly on interviews and direct observations, but rather on information derived from the following sources:

Fernando António Azevedo, *As Ligas Camponesas* (Rio de Janeiro: Paz e Terra, 1982);

Thomas C. Bruneau, *The Political Transformation of the Brazilian Catholic Church* (London: Cambridge University Press, 1974);

Peter Evans, *Dependent Development: The Alliance of Multinational, State, and Local Capital in Brazil* (Princeton, N.J.: Princeton University Press, 1979);

Thomas E. Skidmore, *Politics in Brazil, 1930-1964: An Experiment in Democracy* (New York: Oxford University Press, 1967);

Itamar de Souza, *A Luta da Igreja Contra os Coroneis* (Petrópolis: Vozes, 1982).

[3]When Vargas' military forces reached the city of Rio de Janeiro (which at the time was the capital of Brazil), the incumbent president, Washington Luis, refused to abdicate. At the request of Vargas, it was Cardinal Leme who persuaded Luis to yield. The subsequent alliance formed between the dictator and the cardinal marked the beginning of a new era in Church-state relations in Brazil.

[4]Assistentialism (in Portuguese, *assistencialismo*) is a term commonly used in Brazil to denote what people in the United States would probably call the

social casework approach to the problem of poverty. It usually consists of giving money, food, used clothing and medical aid to people who are unable to work or whose employment does not provide adequate income to support their needs and/or the needs of their families. This concept has recently come under heavy attack by progressive Church people, who point out the injustice of the whole income structure and who advocate replacing assistentialism with social activism aimed toward a more equitable distribution of the wealth that the workers are actually producing for the benefit of the dominant classes.

[5]Spiritism or, more correctly, spiritualism, is a set of practices derived from the belief that it is possible for the dead to communicate with the living. Spiritualism as an organized religion is believed to have originated in France in the nineteenth century with Alain Kardec — hence the term "Kardecism," which is sometimes used to refer to the practice of spiritualism as a cult, with cultic centers and membership (the common form of spiritualism in Brazil), rather than the consultation of individual mediums by individual clients. In Brazil, there are many varieties of religious syncretism, including combinations of folk Catholicism and African and Native American religions, and not all of these include spiritualism. However, in condemning syncretism, Church leaders have tended to term all of its forms "spiritism."

3
SEEDS OF CHANGE
IN THE CHURCH

In order to understand some of the changes that would begin to occur as the result of pastoral responses to new social problems, it is necessary to look first at two Church organizations that would provide important sources of support for those innovations. One of them, Catholic Action, would be a lay movement, and the other would be the National Conference of the Brazilian Bishops (CNBB). Interestingly, it was the lay movement that came first.

I. Catholic Action

Church historians usually refer to two forms of Catholic Action. The earlier Italian model, which was divided into four movements according to age and sex, tended to emphasize traditional, other-worldly piety, and was under the direct control of the local bishop. The other form, which is usually referred to as French, or specialized, Catholic Action, began in the 1920's (although actually in Belgium, not France) with the Young Christian Workers (JOC). The French model divided the lay people into groups that were specialized according to social milieu (to JOC were added movements for students, farmers and middle-class youth — JEC, JAC and JIC, respectively).

The emphasis was on lay spiritual formation and lay leadership in the evangelization of the specific milieux. Invitation to membership in the small Catholic Action cells was extended to persons who appeared to be the natural leaders in their environments. These elite groups of militants came together for prayer, reflection and action. Because of a belief that people's spiritual problems were rooted in bad living conditions, the action was oriented toward social reform, using the method of "See, judge, act." Writings of persons involved in specialized Catholic Action give evidence that a major impetus behind this new approach was a concern about the decline of Church influence over the majority of French and Belgian people and about the spread of socialism among factory workers.[1]

In 1935, Cardinal Leme officially established Brazilian Catholic Action (ACB) according to the Italian form. It was part of his plan to extend the influence of the Church over society.

> Dom Leme saw the necessity for faith to influence society . . . Previously the government had been anti-clerical, but Vargas sought the favor of the Church — a certain type of alliance. So this opened up a potential for the influence of the Church. Dome Leme founded . . . Catholic Action as the apostolate of the laity in the transformation of society.
>
> (Dom Marcelo Cavalheira,
> Bishop of Guarabira, PB)

At the national level, Italian-style Catholic Action never really took hold, although it had temporary success in some regions. By the time Dom Leme died in 1942, the seeds of specialized Catholic Action were already being planted. In that year, French-Canadian missionaries, the Holy Cross Fathers, brought their experience with JEC and JOC to São Paulo and were assisted in the university milieu by Brazilian Dominicans, whose province at that time was still based in France.

> Some persons in Catholic Action sensed a "tiredness" in the general (Italian) form. So they began to adopt the experiences of those priests from French Canada, who talked about the *conversion au réal*. By the 1950's, the influence of JEC, JOC and JUC (University Catholic Action) was stronger than that of general Catholic Action.
>
> (Dom Marcelo Cavalheira)

Meanwhile, in Rio de Janeiro, a group of young factory workers were attempting to organize JOC themselves and were looking for a priest who had enough free time to serve as their chaplain. They recruited a young cleric who had just recently arrived from his home state of Ceará, Father Hélder Câmara.[2] Although Father Câmara did not have previous experience with specialized Catholic Action, he was willing to learn along with the young militants. The latter and their new chaplain were further assisted after 1946 by Father José Távora, who was in contact with the French-Canadian priests in São Paulo.

Father Câmara maintained contact with several groups in Catholic Action and began to feel the necessity to create a national secretariat that could, on the one hand, count on the trust of the bishops and, on the other, coordinate the various branches of Catholic Action on a national level. He was also aware of the ineffectiveness of the Italian-style movement, which was still the official one in Brazil, and he encouraged the formation of groups that were following the inspiration of the French experience. In 1947, at the request of Dom Jaime Câmara, Dom Leme's successor in Rio, Father Hélder Câmara became national chaplain of Catholic Action. With his support, JOC was soon organized on a national level and was followed in 1950 by JAC, JIC, JEC and JUC (in Brazil, there was a separate movement of university students, with JEC reserved for secondary school students). Four years later, the hierarchy approved the specialized movements as the official form of Brazilian Catholic Action.

> In the 1950's, Catholic Action was a pastoral inspira-
> tion, and the emphasis was on forming leaderships
> — social, political, Christian — and on the idea that
> an elite could bring about social change. From this
> inspiration the clergy were shaping their pastoral
> action. It was something that existed in our thinking,
> that the Church should influence the transformation
> of society in the formation of a new culture, by means
> of elites, in all social categories . . . The Church's
> whole mission — educational, pastoral, social — until
> the Second Vatican Council was very much based on
> this presupposition — form elites — that was our
> role — people to create a new society.
>
> (Dom Luiz Fernandes,
> Bishop of Campina Grande, PB)

In the early years of specialized Catholic Action in Brazil, certain features that would profoundly affect the Church were already evident:

(1) Catholic Action validated lay people as Church members with a unique mission;

(2) That mission would orient them toward action for the reformation of their milieux in conformity with Christian social teaching.

> I believe that Brazil, out of all the countries in the
> world, owes very much to Catholic Action, because
> Catholic Action sought to validate the role of the lay

person. It made the laity more responsible for their
place in the Church of Christ . . . And their specific
role is to be a Christian presence in the world.
(Dom Hélder Câmara,
Former Archbishop of Olinda and Recife)

The reorganization of Brazilian Catholic Action from the Italian to the French model provides a clear example of the genesis
of a religious innovation as the result of an interaction between
the hierarchy and people at the grassroots, along with the intervention of priests. French-Canadian missionaries may have
provided an initial stimulus, but, at least in Rio, it was the
young workers who organized themselves and then found a
priest who was willing to learn with and from them. Their
innovation, which was later approved by the bishops, emerged
during a period when new social and pastoral problems were
becoming evident and when the old vehicle for the lay apostolate
was lacking in vitality. So this innovation came about as the
result of lay initiatives, facilitated by sympathetic priests, and
was approved by the higher authorities at a time when the
Church needed some concrete means of adapting to the changing social conditions.

II. The National Conference of the Brazilian Bishops

In the early 1950's Catholic Action was already playing an
important role in the genesis of another organization that would
be decisive in setting future directions for the Church — the
National Conference of the Brazilian Bishops (CNBB). Again
the initiative came from Father Hélder Câmara, with the help
of a group of lay people.

Father Câmara realized that lay people now had national meetings, but that the bishops did not. The

young militants supported his idea for some kind of
national organization for the bishops . . . So originally the CNBB was the idea of Dom Hélder, with
the support of the lay people who, through Catholic
Action, had the means to organize meetings.

(Marina Bandeira,
an active Catholic lay person
and longtime acquaintance of Dom Hélder Câmara)

The general secretariat of Catholic Action took initiatives that afterward helped in the creation of the
National Conference of the Brazilian Bishops
. . . With a country of such extensive dimensions —
almost continental — and a growing number of dioceses, it was necessary to have a secretariat to serve
the bishops of the whole country.

(Dom Hélder Câmara)

It was Father Hélder Câmara (by this time a monseignor)
who expressed the need for a national conference of bishops to
Cardinal Montini (the Vatican Secretary of State, later to become Pope Paul VI). The occasion during which they worked
out the basis for the organization was the World Congress of
the Lay Apostolate held in Rome, in October, 1951. The CNBB
was first organized in 1952. In 1958, it received official approval
from Pope Pius XII.

The first article of the statutes of the CNBB expresses its goal:

With the purpose of studying and discussing — in
meetings of a character that is not conciliar, but
rather cordial — problems in areas of competence of
the episcopacy and of common interest, the National
Conference of the Brazilian Bishops is instituted.

Father Gervasio Queiroga[3] has observed that the formulation of this article was deficient insofar as it did not really express the actual purpose of the CNBB. It was not to be merely a society of academic studies, but rather would have a much more practical function. It would be a means of facilitating a dynamic of permanent renovation and effective coordination of pastoral action for all the dioceses in Brazil.

The CNBB, which anticipated by about ten years *Lumen Gentium* (the document of the Second Vatican Council which provided the basis for national bishops' conferences in other countries), would be a source of official Church support for innovations that would originate in other sectors of the believing community — such as lay people in the poorer classes and in the middle classes, as well as nuns and priests. It would be more than a vehicle for unified responses to social problems and for unified pastoral planning. Under the leadership of some of the most progressive bishops, the national conference would adopt positions and directives far more daring than many of the bishops would have taken on their own. Its official stands would also provide inspiration and ecclesial approval for the work of nuns, priests and lay church workers whose own local bishops might not be very supportive of their efforts at pastoral renewal. Finally, in its bienniel meetings and official documents, the CNBB would serve as a watershed — that is, as a means of consolidating new approaches to the Church's mission in the world and as an impetus to their continuation. When the bishops as a body began to take positions that would lead to the loss of their alliance with the upper classes, it would become virtually impossible for the Church as a whole to turn back to the past.

III. The Beginning of the Natal Movement

The social upheavals of the 1940's were experienced with particular force in Natal, the capital city of Rio Grande do

Norte, located in the northeast sector of the most northeastern state in northeast Brazil.

> The rural exodus was already happening in the 1940's — from the rural areas to Natal, and from Natal to the south of Brazil . . . The migrations were a difficult thing, with people leaving the land and their rural roots.
>
> (Dom António Costa, Auxiliary Bishop of Natal)

In addition to being a way station in the national process of urbanization, Natal was affected by the entry, in 1942, of Brazil into World War II on the side of the United States. The installation of U.S. military bases and the arrival of technicians and North American troops intensified the social disorganization of the area — producing a rise in the cost of living, the introduction of different social customs and mores, an increase in the number of houses of prostitution and a severe housing shortage which resulted in the growth of *favelas*. At the same time, the recruitment of large numbers of laborers for the naval and military bases intensified the patterns of rural-urban migration. The end of the war and the withdrawal of the troops produced an even greater crisis — a sudden rise in unemployment in the face of continued population growth and social disorganization.[4]

The Church's initial response was assistentialism — that is, traditional philanthropic measures taken to try to mitigate the effects of poverty. In 1944, the "First Week of Social Studies of Rio Grande do Norte" drew participants from both the government and the Church, including two young clerics, Father Eugênio Sales and Father Nivaldo Monte. Father Monte, a chaplain for JFC (the young women's sector of general Catholic Action), proposed the formation of a school of social service. This school was begun by members of JFC in 1945, the same year that young men's Catholic Action, JMC, was founded, with Father Sales as its chaplain. In collaboration with the Social Service School of Natal, members of JMC worked at projects of social assistance and catechetics on the urban periphery. In the process of trying to help poor people in the city, the priests and lay workers became aware that the problems resulting from the urban migrations were rooted in the hardships which people suffered in the countryside. They began to form plans for a program of rural assistance.

The archdiocese of Natal may have been somewhat unusual in the vitality of its sectors of general Catholic Action (that is, the Italian model) in the 1940's, and in the fact that the specialized (French-style) movements evolved from them. JFC and JMC became JEC, and the JECists were active in organizing JAC (rural Catholic Action). According to Lourdes Santos, a professor of social welfare and advisor for JEC who began working with Father Sales in 1948:

> Practically everyone in the Natal Movement was from Catholic Action . . . Father Sales asked me to work in the rural milieu, organizing communities and implanting JAC. It was easy to get JAC started, because many of my JECists were daughters of farm workers.

In 1948, with the help of Catholic Actionists, six priests, including Father Sales, Father Monte and Father Expedito Sobral de Medeiros, [5] organized the Rural Assistance Service (SAR — which outside the archdiocese became known as "The Natal Movement"). In spite of its name, SAR soon moved beyond assistentialism.

> We started a center for the training of leaders. Our objective was to get communities organized, for the

purpose of preparing the people to grow, elaborating
programs for the people themselves to solve their
own problems. The leadership courses were begun
in 1949 . . . Part of our work was called the rural
mission. This consisted of a team of volunteers — a
physician, a dentist, an agronomist and one or two
members of JAC — who would donate their time on
weekends. This team would spend two days in one
place. They would arrange meetings in the community for the purpose of getting groups organized.

(Lourdes Santos)

There would be several other programs developed in Natal.
However, many of those later developments will be best under-
stood in relation to rural mobilization that was being done by
people outside the Church. Before looking at this mobilization,
it is important to examine another movement that developed
under the influence of SAR, the Rural Orientation Service of
Pernambuco.

IV. Sorpe

Pernambuco is divided into three regions: The costal area,
the semi-arid *sertão* and the cane-producing *zona da mata*. In
the mid-1950's, the relations of production in the *sertão* were
still semi-feudal, while the cane country was undergoing
capitalization. In 1956, a young JAC chaplain, Father Paulo
Crespo, was appointed pastor in the town of Jaboatão, in the
archdiocese of Olinda and Recife.

The socio-economic situation of the rural workers in
the cane region came as a great surprise to me. It
was different from the region I came from — the
sertão — where the relations between landowners

and workers were more humane, although feudal
. . . So I saw a reality that was very different — the
absolute misery of the cane workers, very poor
dwellings, without beds or tables or anything. Many
of the people were sick. Their wages were miserable.
In those days we priests had a lot of prestige with
the upper classes, the lords of the plantations . . .
But I soon saw that this situation was unjust, for us
as Christians, noting the conditions of the cane
workers.

(Paulo Crespo)

As a JAC chaplain, Father Crespo attended meetings in
Natal. There he noticed the associations set up to defend and
to organize rural workers. Along with some other priests from
Pernambuco, he organized a meeting in Jaboatão of about thirty
people and invited two advisors from Rio Grande do Norte,
Monseignor Expedito and a young lay activist. The participants
at this meeting discussed the social, economic and personal
conditions experienced by the rural workers and agreed that
they were indeed horrifying. They also acknowledged their own
part in the oppressive social structure. Having thus confessed
their guilt, however, their first impulse was still traditional
charity:

We found that we, the priests of the Church, were
still more tied to the landowners than to the workers
— so much so that the first solution that was
suggested at this meeting was that we should work
together with the rich people to get clothing, food
and medicine to give to the workers. But that solution
was rejected after a deeper analysis. We saw that
they were workers and therefore had the right to
receive not merely alms, but a just wage for their
work.

(Paulo Crespo)

So the assistentialist proposal was rejected. Another suggestion was to organize peasant leagues, such as had recently been begun there in Pernambuco with the help of Francisco Julião.[6] But this solution was also rejected

> . . . first of all, because we did not wish to appear to be competing with Julião, creating leagues alongside of his, and secondly, because the peasant league, as a civil association, represented only its own members. We wanted a broader action.
>
> (Paulo Crespo)

The solution finally settled upon was to organize unions of rural workers — a union in each township, federations on the state level and a national confederation of rural workers. Each of the priests who had been present at the meeting in Jaboatão recruited two rural workers to attend a training session. These workers then formed a team that would be responsible for advising other workers on organizing rural unions. This team was named the Rural Orientation Service of Pernambuco (SORPE). SORPE's work was defined according to three phases of organizing:

(1) Unions and federations;

(2) Rural cooperatives;

(3) The political participation of rural workers.

It was clear from the interviews with Paulo Crespo that an important element in the organizing work of SORPE was the presence of clergy who, because of a spiritually based concern for the well-being of their flock, would organize poor people into programs of collective self-help. At the same time, however, another dynamic was operating that would facilitate the acceptance of this new form of Christian charity by some of the more conservative members of the hierarchy.

When we started to organize the unions, it was not
to counteract the peasant leagues. It was to organize
a large movement on the national level to change
radically the situation of the rural workers, in terms
of agrarian reform, social security and a just wage.
Now this is not to say that, in later years, a *few*
priests or bishops did not subscribe to the idea of
SORPE . . . out of fear of the peasant leagues. It
was as though they were saying that it was better
that we organize our own unions, coming from the
Church, with a Christian mentality, than that the
people enter the peasant leagues, which had a
connotation of being "Communist."

(Paulo Crespo)

At the same time the fear of Communism was motivating
some sectors of the conservative hierarchy to support the
actions of innovative clergy, the latter were further developing
their relationship with the rural poor. When the priests began
to question the rural situation, the people began to trust them
and to tell them more — accounts of abusive treatment by the
landowners, imprisonment, torture, death — both shocking
their listeners and leaving these men of the Church amazed at
the simple, unwavering faith that enabled the poor people to
accept their incredible suffering. As the priests continued to
listen and to question, however, the people gradually began to
develop a consciousness of the unjust social roots of their
situation. So, at the grassroots level, there was beginning an
intense process of mutual education between the priests and
the lay people. At the same time, people in the upper classes
were becoming aware of this change in the Church and were
beginning to accuse the clergy of having Communist tendencies.
The cost of the clergy's new relationship with the poor would
be the eventual loss of long-standing alliances with the landed

elite. Thus these early stirrings of the grassroots Church in Pernambuco and in Rio Grande do Norte set in motion a process that would loosen Brazilian Catholicism from its traditional social foundation and set it on a new path that would be both painful and virtually irreversible. This process would be facilitated by a nudge from outside the Church.

NOTES

[1]See Joseph Cardijn, *Challenge to Action* (Chicago: Fides, 1955), pp. 95-96, and John Fitzsimons and Paul McGuire (Eds.), *Restoring All Things: A Guide to Catholic Action* (New York: Sheed and Ward, 1938), p. 166.

[2]Information from an interview with Marina Bandeira (the former national director of the Basic Education Movement and a long-time acquaintance of Dom Hélder Câmara).

[3]Gervásio Fernandes de Queiroga, *CNBB: Comunhão e Corresponsabilidade* (São Paulo: Paulinas, 1977), p. 186.

[4]Cándido Procópio Ferreira de Camargo, *Igreja e Desenvolvimento* (São Paulo: Editora Brasileira de Ciências, 1971), p. 68.

[5]Dom Eugênio Sales later became the acting archbishop of Natal, still later the archbishop of Bahia, and at the time of this writing is the cardinal-archbishop of Rio de Janeiro. Dom Nivaldo is presently archbishop of Natal. Monseignor Expedito is the pastor of São Paulo do Potengí, a rural parish where many of the phases of the Natal Movement were begun as pilot projects. São Paulo do Potengí may have been the location of the first basic ecclesial communities (See Chapter Five).

[6]Francisco Julião's own account of the development of the Peasant Leagues is presented in the next chapter.

4
RURAL MOBILIZATION AND "RED TERROR"

The same political-economic conditions that had helped to generate popular mobilization within the Church were producing a similar phenomenon in the larger society. In addition, the return to a democratic form of government after World War II produced a climate of political openness that would be conducive to social movements in different sectors of Brazilian society — especially students, factory workers and peasants. Among the first to become mobilized were the peasants, and, again, the place was Pernambuco.[1]

A decent burial — it seems to be a fairly simple wish after a life of hard work on land belonging to someone else. However, it was not something that impoverished peasants could take for granted. Frequently they were carried to their final resting place in a borrowed coffin, from which the body was removed just before interment. So in the early 1950's, the tenant farmers of the Galilea Plantation, in the Pernambucan township of Vitória de Santo Antão, decided to form a mutual aid society whose main function would be the pooling of their meager resources for the purchase of simple coffins. They named their organization the "Agricultural Society of Planters and Cattlemen of Pernambuco" (SAPPP) and asked the local landowner, Oscar Beltrão, to be the honorary president.

In spite of this apparently innocuous and non-political beginning, the founding of SAPPP would provide a vehicle for the
exploration of the kinds of problems that peasants usually experienced long before their funerals. The particular threat in
the *zona da mata* was eviction from the land in order to make
way for capital-based cane production. So the tenants of Galilea
began to discuss ways of protecting their right to remain on
the land. They sent representatives to the nearby city of Recife
to find a lawyer to defend their interests.

> They invited me to come to the Galilea Plantation
> to meet with the other people there. And I went.
> About a thousand people received me at the Galilea
> Plantation on January 1, 1955 . . . There I took on
> the commitment of defending them in the courts as
> a lawyer. I also took on the commitment of defending
> them politically, because I was state deputy and was
> able to work through legislative means.
>
> (Francisco Julião)

Francisco Julião had received his law degree from the University of Recife in 1940. During the next several years he represented peasant interests in legal cases involving land tenure,
which influenced the development of his own political ideas.
After World War II, he became affiliated with the Brazilian
Socialist Party, through which he was elected to the state legislative assembly in 1954 (the first Socialist deputy ever elected
in Pernambuco) and to the national assembly in 1958. After
being recruited by the tenant farmers of Galilea and made the
new honorary president of SAPPP (Oscar Beltrão had resigned
from that position as soon as he began to perceive the peasants'
organization as a threat to his property, and tried unsuccess-
fully to dissolve SAPPP), Julião began organizing other associations of peasants. Opponents of the new movement began to

refer to these groups as "peasant leagues," in an attempt to discredit them by means of an implied connection to the leagues organized by the Communist Party during the previous decade. Julião graciously accepted the "compliment," and the name stuck. Before the end of 1955, the leagues had organized the First Peasant Congress of Pernambuco, which drew three thousand tenant farmers and rural wage laborers. It appears that there had occurred the dynamic combination of a charismatic leader and a rural underclass that was ready for change.

As a lawyer and legislator, Julião's efforts were concentrated on enforcing existing legislation and on working toward agrarian reform. As a grassroots organizer, his preferred tactic was the land occupation for the purpose of expropriation of the land for the peasants from the large plantation owners. Through legal means, the tenants of Galilea and of several other *engenhos* (sugar plantations) were able to acquire their own land.

> There were laws against the abuses by the landowners. But it was as though they did not apply in the rural areas, which were still functioning in a semi-feudal system. And so I simply utilized the laws and the constitution . . . I never used illegal measures to defend the peasants, because the laws already existed. I simply applied them.
>
> (Francisco Julião)

The membership of the peasant leagues expanded to include both tenant farmers and rural wage laborers. The leagues quickly spread throughout Pernambuco and the neighboring state of Paraíba, into other parts of the Northeast and then into states in other regions: Rio de Janeiro, Goiás, Paraná, Rio Grande do Sul and Minas Gerais. The largest and strongest leagues were in Pernambuco, Paraíba and Rio de Janeiro.

In terms of members, the growth of the leagues was impressive. Horowitz[3] estimated that they represented about 50,000 peasants by 1958 and between 80,000 and 100,000 by 1960. By the time of the coup in 1964, according to Julião's estimate, there may have been as many as 200,000 members. Clearly they held a strong political potential. As early as 1956, the peasant leagues began to participate in the United Front of Recife, a broad-based coalition of political parties, businessmen, unions and class associations which, in November of that year, organized a general strike to protest new tax measures.

The presidential administrations of the late 1950's and the early 1960's contributed, in a variety of ways, to the unprecedented growth of grassroots movements. Juscelino Kubitschek (1956-61), with his plans for very accelerated industrialization and the building of the new national capital at Brasília, set a tone of national pride, confidence and optimism. Furthermore, because Kubitschek perceived a prosperous rural population to be a potential source of consumers for the expanded domestic industries, he favored agrarian reform. Although what he proposed may be defined as only moderate reform (that is, stopping short of expropriations of the majority of plantations by peasants), his position still provided some hope for the rural poor and a certain encouragement for the peasant leagues.

> Juscelino was the president who adopted a policy of development for the nation — with road construction on a grand scale and new factories. He gave a lot of hope to the industrial bourgeoisie, and that bourgeoisie began to carry a lot of weight in political decisions . . . Elections often would be decided by urban dwellers and no longer by the rural lords. The industrial bourgeoisie was interested in moderate agrarian reform in order to create a rural middle

class that would be capable of purchasing the products of the new industry . . . The government could not oppose what I was doing, because the government itself was creating a new mentality in favor of agrarian reform.

(Francisco Julião)

The political instability of the post-Kubitschek years would contribute in a different way to the further growth and radicalization of the grassroots movements. However, it would also lead to a situation that would eventually produce difficulties for the peasant leagues and new challenges for Julião.

In 1961, the presidential election was won by Jánio Quadros, the candidate of a coalition of opposition parties. Quadros came into office on a platform of social justice, morality and criticism of bureaucratic inefficiency. After seven months of unorthodox actions, conflict with Congress and personal indecisiveness, he abruptly resigned, plunging the country into a political and military crisis.

Although the constitution of 1946 clearly spelled out the succession of the vice president, the military leaders were completely opposed to João Goulart, who at the time was out of the country on an economic mission to the People's Republic of China. The generals viewed Goulart as a labor agitator, a Communist sympathizer and a throwback to the populist manipulations of the Vargas administration. Congress managed to avoid a civil war by proposing a compromise between the opponents of Goulart and the upholders of the constitution: A parliamentary presidency in which the president would have little power. Thus Goulart became president of Brazil. True to his populist reputation, he managed, by means of a plebiscite in January, 1963, to regain full presidential power.[4]

Goulart will probably be remembered as the president who

helped to justify the coup of 1964, because of his political corruption, moral weaknesses, crass populism and blatant courting of the radical left. The political climate during his administration was characterized by confusion, agitation and "red terror." If the high spirits of the Kubitschek administration gave hope to the masses, the resignation of Quadros and the subsequent chaos of the Goulart years helped further to radicalize the grassroots movements by completing the demystification of the system. However, Goulart's talent for manipulation would have negative consequences for the peasant leagues.

Goulart had learned his corporatist[5] lessons well from his mentor, Vargas. His response to a viable grassroots movement was to weaken it by setting up a parallel governmental structure to channel and control the political energy that had helped to produce the movement. So in 1962, he instructed his labor minister to establish a resolution that would specify the norms concerning the organization and recognition of rural unions.

> Since the league was an autonomous movement, it was controlled neither by the state nor by the labor unions of the federal government. It had complete autonomy under civil law. And so, the government, seeking to control it, "created" rural unionization. This was decreed by the government out of a fear that the leagues would continue to grow free from federal control.
>
> (Francisco Julião)

The arrangement was that, in any particular state, the group (for example, Catholic Church, Communist Party or Peasant League) that had the largest number of unions would get to control the state federation. Goulart thus set up a mechanism not only to establish control over the rural movement, but also to divide it. The Church, the Communists and the Peasant

Leagues thus entered into an intense competition for the control over the movement. The Communist Party did not make much headway, leaving most of the competition between the Church and Julião's leagues.

> I founded thirty-six unions. They were called "unions of the league" to distinguish them from unions of the Church. Our unions were much more vigorous, more bold. Those of the Church were more moderate . . . When the military coup came in 1964, the first movement in Brazil that was outlawed . . . was the peasant league. That proves its importance. That proves that the system considered it to be dangerous — because the large landowners supported the coup precisely to eliminate the peasant movement.
>
> (Francisco Julião)

It would appear that the peasant leagues posed a strong challenge to Brazilian society as a whole and in particular to the economic and the political elites, some of whom sought to weaken their influence, others who moved to eliminate them completely. In addition, they also presented a challenge for the Church.

NOTES

[1]Most of the information for this chapter was derived from two tape-recorded interviews with Francisco Julião, supplemented by informal conversations with Dr. Julião, a brief interview and two conversations with another former peasant organizer, and the following books: Horowitz, Irving L., *Revolution in Brazil*, (New York: E.P. Dutton, 1964); Skidmore, Thomas E., *Politics in Brazil, 1930-1964: An Experiment in Democracy*, (New York: Oxford University Press, 1967); Azevedo, Fernando António, *As Ligas Camponesas*, (Rio de Janeiro: Paz e Terra, 1982).

[2]Azevedo, *op. cit.*, pp. 60-62.

[3]Horowitz, *op. cit.* p. 22.

[4]See Skidmore, *op. cit.,* pp. 187-302, for a discussion of the presidential administrations of Quadros and Goulart.

[5]Corporatism is the organization of interests groups into vertical categories controlled by a strong central government — in contrast to horizontal groups, such as class associations. James M. Malloy, in *Authoritarianism and Corporatism in Latin America* (Pittsburg: University of Pittsburg Press, 1977) defines corporatism as "a system of interest representation based on enforced limited pluralism." The governmental funding and regulation of trade unions is one example of the nature and consequences of corporatism (See Chapter Six of this book). All autonomous pressure groups that might pose a threat to the centralized power structure are neutralized by this system of vertical control. Vargas' alliance with Cardinal Leme in the 1930's was another example of corporatism, since it represented a fairly successful means of controlling the Church's function of legitimating ideas and values, which, in this case, were used to support Vargas' dictatorship.

5
FURTHER SOCIAL AND PASTORAL INNOVATIONS

It should be evident from Chapter Three that the efforts of Church people toward the amelioration of social problems were at least partly motivated by a sincere concern for the poor. There is no denying, however, that the fear of Communism, especially as symbolized by Julião and the peasant leagues, also influenced the actions of some of the priests and the bishops. This combination of motives was well described by the auxiliary bishop of Natal during an interview in which he was talking about the rural unions begun by SAR in the early 1960's:

> Then there were the peasant leagues, whose leader was said to be "red," Marxist, Communist . . . This was not the only reason the Church was concerned about strengthening the rural unions. However, Pope Pius IX did say that the Church had lost the (industrial) working class and must not also lose the rural class.
>
> (Dom António Costa)

A similar explanation was given by Monseignor Expedito Sobral de Medeiros, pastor of São Paulo do Potengí. It is interesting to note some similarities in the explanations of the situation given by Julião and Monseignor Expedito, persons who in the 1950's and 1960's likely held opposing views:

> The Church took a conservative position. In some cases it was even hostile. It saw Communists everywhere. And it offered resistance to political and social organizations that could take away a certain leadership that it exercised in the society. However, the Church evolved. Today it is more than tolerant. It is participating (in the people's struggle).
>
> (Francisco Julião)

> We became conscious of the problems of the rural classes, who appeared to have been completely abandoned. We were also motivated by a certain fear of the peasant leagues. They were seen as Communist and had been organized by Francisco Julião — you've heard of him? — Today we would not do what we did then, because now he is doing good things. But then it appeared that he was using that work for his own political goals.
>
> (Monseignor Expedito)

In these interviews just quoted, Julião and a representative of the Church seemed to be trying to communicate a respect for each other's present work. They also presented each other as having changed in some way from an earlier tendency toward political manipulation, although, interestingly, neither seemed to perceive such a change in his own position. To an outside observer, it would appear that, twenty-five years earlier, Julião and the Church had been in competition for the loyalty of the people. The concern of the clergy at that time was that rural people would fall into atheism unless they utilized Christian social teachings in searching for solutions to their problems.

I. Further Developments in Natal

The archdiocese of Natal, whatever were the motives of its bishops and priest, continued through the early 1960's to be in a position of leadership in the development of Brazilian Catholic social action. One catalyst in the advancement of its social role was the drought of 1958.

> There was the usual local corruption over government aid, and the people were not able to get the food that they needed. Dom Eugênio [Father Sales had become an archbishop] saw what was happening. He went to the local officials and demanded that the food supplies be distributed to the people. After this, the groups organized by the Church took over the distribution of government relief supplies. This situation led to the conscientization of the people in relation to the need for cooperatives, which began one or two years later.
>
> (Lourdes Santos)

People working in SAR began organizing farmers' cooperatives in 1960 and rural unions shortly afterward. The strategy was to implant the unions first in the regions nearest to Paraíba, aiming to occupy immediately those areas that would likely be worked by the peasant leagues.[1] The Catholic union movement quickly spread to other northeast states. Unlike the peasant leagues, however, the Church unions did not advocate the redistribution of large land holdings to the peasants, but rather tended to restrict their demands to better wages and working conditions for rural laborers. Nevertheless, the large landowners would still accuse Dom Eugênio of being a Communist agent.

Another of SAR's social programs that would spread to other

areas was its system of radio schools. These combined literacy, grassroots education and a variety of social and religious programs.

> We began to see that rural problems were related to the lack of basic education. So Dom Eugênio went to Sutatenza, Colombia, to observe the radio schools . . . He got the radio transmitter in 1958. People would pool their resources and buy one radio for the whole village. It would be set up in a community center. There were radio programs for each community group, and, at the appropriate time, the group would gather for its program, for example, JAC, youth club, mothers' club, health education, catechism — there was also Mass over the radio. Later we added radio programs for cooperatives and rural unions. We needed to have monitors for the courses. Leaders emerged from the communities themselves.
>
> (Lourdes Santos)

This description of the experience of the radio schools in Natal evokes an image of little groups of people in isolated rural villages, gathered around a radio with a local leader, developing their faith, their ability to read and write and their social consciousness. The influence of the archdiocese was assured by the fact that the radios were set up to tune into one station only.

The concept of the radio schools quickly spread to other dioceses. Similar programs were established in the northeast dioceses of Crato, Penedo and Aracajú, as well as in other regions of the country. The experience of Natal influenced other dioceses in the northeast through both formal and informal channels of communication. One formal channel was the regional meeting.

II. Church, State, and Rural Development Projects

The first regional meeting of the bishops of the northeast was held in Campina Grande, Paraíba in May, 1956. Dom Eugênio Sales and Dom Hélder Câmara had been influential in organizing this gathering, which was particularly significant as the first attempt by the bishops to coordinate pastoral and social efforts on a regional level. It was also significant in terms of creating a foundation for Church-state cooperation in projects of social reform. The event was attended by President Kubitschek, who stated that he did not see anything out-of-place about a group of bishops meeting to discuss the social and economic development of their region. One of the president's contributions was the furnishing of all available data on the region, so that discussions could proceed with full understanding of the reality. From the Campina Grande meeting came the proposal for OPENE (Operation Northeast), which would form the basis for SUDENE (Superintendency for the Development of the Northeast), a government-funded program for coordinating all economic development projects in the region.

In 1959 Dom Eugênio invited twenty-five bishops and several government officials for a second meeting in Natal. Apparently not all of the government's promises had been fulfilled, because Dom Hélder had this to say to Kubitschek:

> Sir, if you cannot accomplish forty points, do not promise fifty; if you cannot accomplish thirty, do not promise forty; if you cannot come up with twenty, do not promise thirty; if you cannot attend to ten, do not promise twenty; if you cannot deliver five, do not promise ten; and if you cannot fulfill anything, Mr. President, do not promise anything, because the people of the northeast are already tired of hearing the promises of political demoagogues.[2]

SUDENE went through. It was to be more than a basis for
the development of the northeast. It also provided a model for
Church-state cooperation that would be further utilized in the
area of education.

III. The Basic Education Movement (MEB)

As a result of positive experiences with the radio schools in
Natal and other dioceses, some of the bishops began to think
in terms of a larger-scale grassroots education movement. With
the precedent already set for Church-state cooperation in
SUDENE, it was logical to request that the federal government
finance such a project. In November 1960, Dom José Távora
presented to the central commission of the CNBB a proposal
which drew unanimous approval. The proposal called for a
nationwide network of radio schools, for which the government
would provide the financing and the CNBB would provide the
personnel and the administration. On November 11, 1960, Dom
Távora brought the proposal to the newly elected president,
Jánio Quadros. On March 21, 1961, Quadros signed a decree
that established the Basic Education Movement (MEB), with
the help of over four hundred million cruzeiros.[3]

The CNBB was not the only nation-wide Catholic organization with a key role in MEB. Besides the bishop-directors and
the local monitors (selected from the local community), almost
all of the people were past or present Catholic Action militants.

> JUCists and JECists were in the majority of people
> working in MEB, including the animation teams that
> went out to the rural areas to organize the local
> groups.
> (Marina Bandeira, National Director of MEB)

It is interesting to note that the influence of the CNBB and of Catholic Action were not completely separate:

> The Basic Education Movement was largely the initiative of bishops who had been chaplains in Catholic Action — for example, Dom José Távora — and also involved lay people from Catholic Action
> . . . The influence of Catholic Action in the CNBB was evident in the leadership of Dom Hélder.
> (A former JUCist and MEB staff member)

The question of the sources of influence in the development of MEB, and of its method of conscientization, is a complex one. There are at least three levels of influence which must be considered:

(1) the general idea of having such a program;

(2) the practical methodology utilized at the grassroots level;

(3) the overall philosophy of the personnel.

The general idea clearly came from Natal. However, there were differences of philosophy between MEB and SAR. MEB sought involvement in the changing secular milieu, while SAR was to some extent a defense against radical social change. There were practical consequences to these ideological differences. Two different interviewees indicated that Dom Eugênio had opposed the entry of JUC and of MEB into his archdiocese.

> The Natal Movement was marked by Church authority. It was an attempt to absorb movements from outside the Church. The orientation of MEB was closer to that of JUC. It was the view of the Church as present in the world . . . People from MEB and JUC were prevented from participating in the Natal Movement.
> (A former MEB staff member from the Northeast)

> The Natal Movement challenged many of the old
> structures, but stopped short of socialism . . . Dom
> Eugênio prevented JUC from entering Natal in 1961
> and blocked MEB in 1962, even then showing a
> certain resistance to action committed to real social
> change.
> (A former JUCist and MEB staff member from São
> Paulo)

These statements seem to suggest that any linkage between
SAR and MEB was limited to the level of the general idea of
the program. Although some interviewees suggested that the
original motive for starting MEB may have been anti-
Communist (as was the motive for starting some of the
programs in SAR), they also stated or implied that MEB soon
developed a more radical position. It may be relevant to note
that the originators of SAR had had experience with the
traditional clerical Italian form of Catholic Action, whereas
MEB people were familiar with the French/Belgian model of
the specialized movements, such as JUC and JEC, which were
in the process of developing in radical political directions (as
will be described in Chapter Seven). Furthermore, since SAR
was limited to one diocese, it could retain a clerical orientation
because of the likelihood that a local program could remain
under the tight control of the bishop. MEB, on the other hand,
was a national program with lay people in its directorate,
allowing for just a little more freedom to develop a new
orientation.

> MEB had a series of great privileges in relation to
> the CNBB, especially with Dom Távora, who was
> very enthusiastic. The bishops not only began to
> allow the lay people to do more, but they also began
> to believe in the lay people.
> (A MEB state director)

Nevertheless, the influence of Catholic Action on MEB was subtle, and was not the first thing mentioned in interviews with former MEB directors and staff members when asked about the origins of its methodology.

> MEB was trying something totally new. We did what we thought was right and what we could do, and left the solutions up to the people. The concept of conscientization was developed within MEB around 1962. Nobody was conscious of coining a new term. It simply emerged as a word that was descriptive of what we were trying to do — to encourage the poor to say what they wanted, and then to discuss it among themselves and with us in a situation of mutual education.
>
> (Marina Bandeira)

> There was a political problem that delayed the radio license in our area. So, while waiting for it, we put aside literacy work and began discussing with the people themselves what they thought should be done. So the program of grassroots education had strong imput from the rural poor people themselves.
> (A former JUCist and MEB staff member from Maranhão)

> The Catholic Action method of see-judge-act influenced MEB. But our method was also developed through actual practice.
> (A former JECist and MEB staff member from Maranhão)

Since the MEB staff were almost all Catholic Action militants and the key bishops were former chaplains, it is likely that the see-judge-act method was part of their experience and of their common sense. Consequently, they may not have even been fully conscious of the extent of its influence. It seems plausible that their Catholic Action background had predisposed them to develop an action-reflection approach, and may have been the very factor that led them to be open to learning from the people.

In any case, the influence of Catholic Action on MEB was not so much in relation to specific pedagogical techniques. Rather this influence was more in terms of general philosophy. Both MEB's method of conscientization and the "see-judge-act" of Catholic Action involved action and reflection in small groups with non-directive leaders. Both encouraged transforming the social milieu. The main difference between the two methods was in the population invited to use them. While Catholic Action was oriented toward the spiritual-social formation of a militant elite, MEB's method was for the people at the grassroots. The practical application of conscientization is evident in the following selections from the MEB primer, *Viver é Lutar, (To Live is to Struggle):*

I live and struggle.
Pedro lives and struggles.
The people live and struggle.
I, Pedro and the people live.
I, Pedro and the people struggle.
We struggle to live.
To live is to struggle.

(First Lesson)

The peasant is a man of the land.
He works the land.
He gathers the fruits of the land.
Does the peasant have land?

Does he have all he needs to cultivate the land?
Does he have a guarantee of the harvest?
Does the peasant have any guarantee of work?
(Sixteenth Lesson)

The peasants feel the need for unity.
They feel that united they can take action.
Their right to unity is lawful.
Pedro and his fellow workers want to start a union.
A union is unity.
A union is strength.
Unity creates strength in the union.
(Twenty-first Lesson)

MEB was begun only three years before the coup. In 1964, many JUCists were imprisoned or forced to leave the country, considerably changing the composition of the MEB staff. In addition *Viver é Lutar* was replaced by a more conventional primer. Finally, funding was progressively reduced. A brief note in the *Brazilian Ecclesiastical Review* in December 1967, revealed the difficulties faced by MEB. Because of "financial and other restrictions," the program had already been reduced by two-thirds since 1963.

By the late 1960's MEB had died. But its influence went far beyond the duration of its existence.

MEB created a mentality, a climate, an aspiration. Its influence resulted in the formation of many unions and cooperatives. People learned how to participate, how to take initiatives.
(A former JUCist and MEB staff member
from Maranhão)

MEB conscientized the rural workers. This was an

important change. People wanted to take on more.
They wanted to be responsible for working in their
own community — especially through rural unions.
                                    (A priest from Maranhão)

The Church was moving away from assistentialism
and toward a greater social consciousness. MEB
played an important role in developing this new
consciousness.
                        (A MEB staff member from Pernambuco)

In the northeast, MEB was a germinating nucleus.
MEB helped people look at social problems and
discuss them. It created a climate of discussion and
community.
                        (A former priest from Pernambuco)

In summary, MEB's influence remained both in the rural
communities and in the Church. In the former, the results were
seen in unions, cooperatives and a general spirit of
communitarian self-help. For the latter, the consequences
included further validation of a strong lay role and the opening
toward the world begun with specialized Catholic Action.
Finally, the concept of conscientization would become a
permanent part of the Church's terminology, even finding its
way into the pastoral plans of the CNBB and into the everyday
life of the basic ecclesial communities that would emerge later.[4]

IV. Creative Approaches to Pastoral Problems

At the same time that the Brazilian Catholic Church was
opening out to the world, it was also looking within itself to
find more effective methods of evangelizing the nation's
changing population. Many of these efforts began as a means

of dealing with the shortage of clergy in the face of apparent increases in adherents to Protestantism and "spiritism." However, much more positive than this initial motive was the end result of many of the measures taken — a greater value placed on the role of the laity as representing a distinctive position within the Church community. MEB had involved lay people in the Church's social projects. Other innovations would expand this lay role into pastoral functions.

1. BARRA DO PIRAI

One of the anecdotal accounts of pastoral innovations in the 1950's begins with the story of the pious woman in the diocese of Barra do Pirai, RJ, who approached her bishop, Dom Agnelo Rossi, with this complaint:

> At Christmas, the three Protestant churches were lighted and full of people. We could hear their hymns . . . And our Catholic Church was closed, in darkness . . . Why don't we get any priests?
> (Quoted in Salem, 1981: 155)

Out of a concern for finding a practical means of defending the faith before the Protestant threat, Dom Rossi came up with the idea of training "popular catechists" to keep the parishes going in the absence of clergy. However, the limits of the role were sharply defined. Although the catechists were very carefully selected and rigorously trained, they had to adhere strictly to printed materials distributed by the diocese.

> The popular catechist reads and does not speak. He is a lector, not a preacher or an improvisor.
> (Dom Agnelo Rossi[5])

The format given to the catechist included hymns, prayers and the Scriptural readings for the particular Sunday, with pre-packaged commentary. Although it was admittedly a highly restricted lay role, this practice of "Sunday-without-priest" would spread to other dioceses and would eventually be adapted by the basic ecclesial communities in a manner that would give greater freedom to the lay people in discussing Scripture.

2. SÃO LUIS

In the late 1950's and early 1960's, the archdiocese of São Luis (Maranhão) was the location of pastoral innovations. At the time, the archbishop was Dom José Delgado, who had previously been bishop of Caicó (near Natal, in Rio Grande do Norte), in the 1940's and early 1950's. His auxiliary bishop was Dom António Fragoso, who had been a Catholic Action chaplain.

> Dom Delgado saw that priests kept repeating the same sacramental tasks and decided to bring about a change in pastoral action. Between 1952 and 1963, he subdivided the parishes into chapels. Dom António Fragoso organized three-day training meetings for lay people from the chapels. Dom Delgado had a good pastoral sense. With the creation of the chapels, the lay peole had to do more. With the three-day meetings they got their chance . . . Dom Fragoso was in close contact with all the groups. He stimulated participation at the grassroots and created in the priests a questioning of the traditional pastoral approaches.
>
> (A priest from Maranhão)

> Dom Delgado was very effective pastorally, and very supportive of both Catholic Action and MEB. It was he who invited the lay people to organize MEB in Maranhão.
>
> (A former JUCist and MEB staff member from Maranhão)

With encouragement from Dom Delgado and Dom Fragoso, priests in Maranhão began experimenting with new pastoral approaches — popular catechists, JAC, ACR (rural Catholic Action for adults) and basic ecclesial communities. As the rural chapels evolved into basic communities, the title of the catechist was changed to "animator." The communities used the method of conscientization and developed both a political sense and a strong lay role in religious ritual and Scriptural reflection. Priests helped to facilitate the development of the new lay roles.

> (The priests were) just one part of the total context that led to the development of the basic communities. Some of them started out as fairly traditional priests, but they evolved. (They) seemed to become converted at the same time that people in MEB were developing their program.
> (A former JUCist and MEB staff member)

> The beginning of the basic communities in this area came with the transfer of Father J. from (another place), where he had been doing similar work . . . He created a people's directorate — a group of six people chosen by the community. He started meeting with this directorate, providing them with orientation.
> (A member of a basic community)

These quotes illustrate a range of roles for priests in interaction with people at the grassroots. Some started out in traditional clerical roles and changed along with the people. Others arrived in a community with a method which they were ready to use in order to stimulate lay participation. These differences may also reflect a time lapse. In the late 1950's and early 1960's, priests and sisters were experimenting with new pastoral forms. By the middle-to-late sixties, these experiments had begun to crystallize into methods which could be learned and applied as means of engaging poor people in both religious participation and social action.

In 1963 Dom José Delgado became archbishop of Fortaleza, and the following year Dom António Fragoso was made bishop of Crateús. Since that time the archdiocese of São Luis and several other dioceses in Maranhão that grew out of it have not exactly been known for the presence of progressive bishops. However, the continued vitality of lay leadership in Maranhão even up to the present time is a testimony to the efforts of the former archbishop, his auxiliary and the clergy and sisters who worked under their inspiration. In addition, the influence of Dom Delgado extended beyond São Luis through his active role in the National Conference of the Brazilian Bishops in the 1950's and 1960's.[6]

3. MOVEMENT FOR A BETTER WORLD

The Movement for a Better World (MMM), which came to Brazil from Italy, played an important part in renewal within the Church. It consisted mainly of a pedagogical team that went all over the country giving courses to priests, sisters and lay people, in order to orient them toward the adaptation of the Church's pastoral approach to the demands of the modern world. Thus the MMM prepared the Brazilian Catholic Church to be receptive to new ideas that would be embodied in Vatican II. Some of the Brazilian clergy were particularly affected by this spirit of pastoral renewal, as is indicated by this description by a missionary sister of the priests who taught at the Intercultural Formation Center (CENFI — a language and culture school for missionaries entering Brazil) in Petrópolis:

All these men who were directing the Center had a great understanding of the possible outcome of Vatican II. They introduced us almost immediately to some very innovative ideas, like telling us, for example, that Mass would be said in the vernacular. We had never heard of such nonsense! . . . When we went into the chapel in Petrópolis, they had taken out the pews. It looked as though they weren't encouraging us to do much kneeling.

The Movement for a Better World was begun in Italy by Father Ricardo Lombardi with the encouragement of Pope Pius XII. Although MMM courses were begun in Brazil in the late 1950's by Father José Marins, the movement really took hold in 1960, when Father Lombardi came to Brazil to preach a retreat to the bishops. He succeeded in convincing many of them to encourage the courses in their dioceses. Between 1960 and 1965, over twelve hundred Better World courses had been given to approximately five thousand persons.[7] The movement encouraged working in pastoral teams, applying the scientific principles of planning to pastoral work and attempting unified pastoral planning on the diocesan level. It also resulted in stronger ecclesial roles for lay people and for nuns, a sense of community and cooperation and pastoral experiments aimed at the revitalization of parishes.

In summary, the Movement for a Better World generated a spirit of Church renewal and was a contributing factor in the development of the CNBB's pastoral plans of 1962 and 1965.

4. NÍZIA FLORESTA

One of the measures inspired by the Movement for a Better World was the Nízia Floresta experiment in the Archdiocese of Natal. This experiment was begun as another means of dealing with the shortage of clergy. This time it would be religious sisters who filled the gap. Nízia Floresta was the first parish to be run by nuns (as it still is today), and it provided a model that would be adopted in other priest-short areas. The sisters' functions were defined as:

(1) assuming all parish duties, *except* those specifically defined as priestly (such as saying Mass);

(2) maintaining the living Christian faith;

(3) creating a sense of parish community;

(4) seeing that the lay people assume an active role in the Church.

There was a numerical logic in this measure. With five times as many sisters as priests (See Appendix IV), it made sense to utilize their services in direct pastoral work, thus offering them an alternative to teaching in private schools. In addition, some of the functions listed above indicate that the acceptance of a more active role for nuns would help to create a more active role for lay people as well. In this way Nízia Floresta helped to prepare the way for the basic ecclesial communities.

5. BASIC ECCLESIAL COMMUNITIES (CEBs)

In Brazil at the present time, there are estimated to be as many as one hundred thousand basic ecclesial communities — small, lay-led communities of faith that combine Scriptural reflection with social action — but no one seems to be certain as to exactly where they began. The archdiocese of São Paulo has the largest number, but they did not begin there until the late 1960's. People in Maranhão say that CEBs have existed there for at least twenty years, and this claim is supported by written records of regional meetings of CEB representatives that have been held every year since January, 1965.[8] It is possible that even the term "basic community" may have originated there. Also, as was indicated by an earlier quote, parish decentralization and the training of lay catechists were begun in the archdiocese of São Luis in the early 1950's. However, there is similar evidence of early beginnings of basic ecclesial communities in the archdiocese of Natal.

> With the radio programs, people began to grow in the dimension of communitarian faith. They were already people of faith, but now this faith took on a more communitarian aspect. They spontaneously started mutual aid and meetings of "Sunday-with-out-priest." The leaders who emerged from the community were responsible for this new dimension of faith, including the preparation of people for the reception of the sacraments.
>
> (Lourdes Santos)

Within the archdiocese of Natal, it may be possible to pinpoint the beginning of the basic ecclesial communities even more precisely in the "pilot parish"[9] of São Paulo do Potengí.

> Parish decentralization started in São Paulo do Potengí in the 1950's. It was a practical necessity. It was impossible for one priest to minister to all those people. Look at this map. This parish has an area of over one thousand square kilometers, and has over forty thousand people. I had to "make do" somehow. So it was necessity that led me to look for (lay) leaders. And so a type of community emerged at that time.
>
> (Monseignor Expedito)

There are certain social and religious similarities between these two milieux where the basic communities seem to have first emerged. Both areas were rural and characterized by widespread poverty rooted in great inequalities in land-ownership — that is, these were areas where the process of conscientization would be likely to take root if facilitated by sisters and

priests trusted by the people. Both were areas that were ripe
for pastoral innovations — priest-short dioceses where there
were innovative auxiliary bishops who had been Catholic Action
chaplains. Furthermore, it is possible that there had been some
sharing of ideas between bishops in the two dioceses. Although
São Luis and Natal are about a thousand miles apart, Dom
José Delgado had previously been bishop of Caicó, which is not
far from Natal, until 1952; thus it is possible that he was in
contact with Dom Eugênio Sales during the very time period
when the latter was a young priest involved in starting SAR.
In any case, whether the basic ecclesial communities began
first in Maranhão or in Rio Grande do Norte, they had a very
small beginning. They were just one part of the political and
religious ferment around 1960 and would not become visible
on a national level for another decade. Later the CEBs would
represent the Church's belated entry into the popular movements. Meanwhile, those secular movements would continue
to grow without help from the Church.

NOTES

[1]Itamar de Souza, *A Luta da Igreja Contra os Coroneis* (Petrópolis: Vozes,
1982), p. 58.

[2]Quoted in Souza, *op. cit.,* pp. 35-36.

[3]*Revista Eclesiástica Brasileira* 21, 2 (1961), pp. 496-497.

[4]The early emergence of the basic ecclesial communities (CEBs) will be described in Part IV of this chapter. The CEBs will be further discussed in
Chapters Nine and Eleven.

[5]Quoted in Faustino Luiz Couto Texeira, *Comunidade Eclesial de Base:
Elementos Explicativos de sua Génese* (Unpublished Master's Thesis, Depart-
ment of Theology, Catholic University of Rio de Janeiro, 1982), p. 56.

[6]Information derived from an interview with Monseignor Expedito Sobral
de Medeiros.

[7]Texeira, *op. cit.,* p. 64.

[8]The existence of regional gatherings by the beginning of 1965 would seem to indicate that basic communities were already there for at least a year or two.

[9]I have referred to São Paulo do Potengí as the "pilot parish" because many of the phases of the Natal Movement were tried there first.

6
THE BRAZILIAN REVOLUTION: POPULAR STYLE

Some of the factors that created the climate conducive to the flourishing of popular movements have already been discussed — industrialization, urbanization, rural capitalization and the sense of optimism that was characteristic of the Kubitschek years. After 1960, however, the mobilization began to intensify. Jánio Quadros tried to break away from the compromise politics of previous presidents, giving many people hope that government could be different. In addition, his maverick foreign policy helped to provide a favorable climate for anti-imperialist ideology. Then Quadros' abrupt resignation and the absence of a strong presidency during the first fifteen months of Goulart's administration helped to create a sense of drift, which was favorable to the emergence of radical movements seeking to break away from past political structures.[1] The populist stance of the dominant politicians of the 1960's served to encourage further mobilization of various sectors of the population — particularly peasants, factory workers and students.

The very experience of the popular mobilization during the crisis following Quadros' resignation, itself had a further mobilizing effect. The threat of a coup to block Goulart's presidency brought about a great deal of resistance, coming from politicians and some segments of the military as well as from organized labor, students, and the rural movements. With the restoration of Goulart's full presidential powers,[2] combined with the attention which Goulart gave to labor leaders, there was the sense, until 1964, that the popular classes were gaining social and political power. Many middle-class activists believed that those classes were going to rise up very soon and saw their role as accelerating the process, by deepening people's politicization.[3] This was the context for the intensification of popular mobilization.

I. Rural Movements

Much of what was happening with popular mobilization in general had already occurred in the rural milieu — that is, a radical movement with a more moderate parallel in the Church. By 1962, the Church's unions were beginning to eclipse the peasant leagues, a process that was accelerated by Goulart's decree that established rural unions under government control. Nevertheless, the leagues were still very visible and were becoming a political force. After the National Peasants' Congress, held in November of 1961, there was an intensification of grassroots activity in rural areas. Violence became more frequent in the confrontations between plantation owners and peasants attempting to take over land, and between legal squatters on state-owned land and speculators who were trying to establish false claims. National congressmen, many of whom owed their political positions to the large landowners, became concerned about, and opposed to, this rural groundswell.[4] This opposition would have negative consequences for the Church's unions. Although religious leaders may have encouraged their formation for a mixture of reasons, which included both a concern for the well-being of the workers and a fear of Communism, these unions would be identified by many politicians, landowners and journalists with the peasant leagues. As a result, the Church-led unions would be perceived as a threat to the social order.

> So many league members joined unions that the landowners started to say that the two were the same and that the unions were Communist. The bourgeois press, which was already preparing the public opinion to accept the coup, began to present all rural organizing as the same thing and Francisco Julião as public enemy number one.
>
> (Paulo Crespo)

Clearly the battle lines were being drawn. The very unions which had been established in opposition to a Communist threat were now being perceived as part of that threat. Meanwhile, there were other popular movements that were also contributing to this atmosphere of imminent revolution.

II. Labor

The urban labor movement was an interesting combination of autonomous action and the use of the state apparatus. The corporative structure that had been set up by Vargas continued to provide for the government funding of unions, the settling of disputes in labor courts and the prohibition of strikes. In the 1950's and 1960's, radical labor leaders did not attempt to change this arrangement but rather used the government unions as a power base to influence national policy. They did this by controlling important sources of patronage and policy within their official government positions, as well as by the threat of illegal strikes.[5]

The early 1960's saw the growth of labor federations that were relatively free from direct state control. Their non-legal position did not prevent them from functioning as civil associations or from organizing the working class as a political force. The consequent weakening of the state's control over the unions gave the labor leaders even more flexibility in their tactics. Not surprisingly, the anti-strike laws were honored more in the breach than in the observance. The early 1960's were the most intensive period of strike activity in over thirty years. Between 1961 and 1962 alone, there were 334 strikes in São Paulo.[6] These included strikes in individual industries over particular labor issues as well as general strikes over political issues, such as the presidential succession in 1961.

The autonomous labor federations represented the beginning of the organizational unification of the working class. Among the federations was the General Confederation of Workers (CGT), whose political power was derived from its capacity to paralyze economic activity nation-wide and "to touch off the explosive force of the urban mob."[7] The CGT, which was begun by radical labor militants in 1962, would provide the greatest challenge to Goulart's power over the unions. Since he perceived this federation as powerful, he not only utilized its power within his political base but also made an unsuccessful attempt to divide that power. Goulart tried to undermine the CGT by giving state support to the UST, another autonomous federation that was founded in São Paulo in 1962. This ploy backfired when he discovered that the most powerful labor leaders were all in the CGT. Goulart's subsequent attempts to renew his ties with the latter further increased the CGT's bargaining power with the president.

III. The Military

Between 1960 and 1963, the military tended to be in support of the labor strikes. This proved useful to labor, since the governors of the states of São Paulo and Rio de Janeiro were very hostile to the radical labor movement and often used police force to crush strikes. Since these were the two states with the largest numbers of urban workers, the support of the military was important to the strikers.

In 1963, however, the position of the higher military shifted from active support of the strikes (or at least benevolent neutrality) to a position of hostility. At this point, labor leaders sought the support of sergeants and non-commissioned officers. As a result of this contact with radical labor, the lower military themselves became more activist. In September 1963, several hundred non-commissioned officers and enlisted men of the Marines, Air Force and Navy staged an unsuccessful revolt in Brasília, attempting to seize control of the government. The revolt failed because of poor coordination but, nevertheless, had far-reaching political consequences. Goulart's failure to take a definite position on the event weakened the confidence of the higher military and would help set the stage for the coup.

IV. Students

The National Student Union (UNE), which was financed by a subsidy from the government's Ministry of Education, seems to have been another example of corporative structure that threatened to get away from the government's control. In the 1950's, key positions began to be held by Communist youth, who began to be replaced in the early 1960's by JUCists.

> In 1961 a militant of JUC became national President of UNE. Once JUCists got involved in the UNE, they very quickly took over elected positions, first locally, then nationally, replacing Communist students.
> (A former JUCist)

Involvement in social movements was nothing new for the

UNE and did not begin only with the JUCist infiltration. Since the end of World War II, students had been involved in campaigns for amnesty for political prisoners, the national exploitation of oil, the democratization of political institutions and educational reform. After 1960, they began to promote basic social changes, which included both university reform and land reform.[8]

The student activists believed that the best means for the politicization of the masses would be the working out of problems in relation to each different milieu. In other words, each sector of the population should become aware of structural problems through the struggle in relation to its own immediate concerns — for example, workers through their economic claims, peasants through the struggle for land and students through university reform. Given this analysis, it was not suprising that one of the aims of the UNE was to increase the peasant-worker-student alliance. One of the vehicles used by the UNE to build this alliance was the Popular Culture Center.

V. Popular Culture

Within the general climate of the orientation toward popular culture and the use of the arts as a socially critical force, two organizations stand out: The Popular Culture Movement (MCP) in Recife and the Popular Culture Center (CPC) in Rio de Janeiro. The MCP provided the inspiration for the CPC.

The Popular Culture Movement was begun in 1961 by a group of intellectuals in Pernambuco. Although a non-governmental association, it received financial support from the city and state government, particularly from the Secretariat of Education of Recife. With this funding, the MCP developed activities in popular art and education in the schools, community groups, an art gallery, a cultural center and "culture squares," where public productions were presented. Its adult literacy program in the interior of Pernambuco was based on the pedagogical method of Paulo Freire,[9] who was one of the founders of MCP. In addition to literacy, the arts and artisanry, MCP also sponsored medical clinics, health education and courses in auto mechanics, radio installation, sewing, typing and grassroots education (conscientization). This last element linked cultural education to the integration of the rural people into the process of national liberation. Thus the central objective of the Popular Culture Movement was "education for freedom."[10]

The objective of the Popular Culture Center (CPC) was likewise to help create attitudes favorable to people's political participation, by means of an educational program "to open possibilities of transforming reality."[11] Unlike MCP, the CPC received no government funding. Funded by a group of theater people in Rio, it established strong ties with the National Student Union, to the mutual benefit of the two organizations. UNE provided space for the CPC, and the latter helped UNE to reach out to the masses of students.

In attempting to reach out to the working class on the periphery of Rio, however, the CPC ran into two difficulties:

(1) Carlos Lacerda, the conservative governor of Rio, sent the police to disrupt their performances;

(2) they did not find the workers where they had expected to — in the unions. Performances held on union premises were not attended.

These two difficulties led CPC members to develop the technique of street theatre in the form of short sketches. In addition to working on the city streets and in the universities, CPC people used drama as a vehicle for political education in rural villages in the interior of the state of Rio de Janeiro.

In addition to drama, CPC later developed work in the areas

of cinema, music, fine arts, architecture, literature and adult literacy.[12]

VI. Reflections

It is difficult, solely by means of a collection of descriptions of different movements, to capture a sense of the experience of the 1961-1964 period in Brazil and of how that experience was perceived within the Church. Two very different perceptions of the overall political and religious context are evident in the following excerpts from interviews with North Americans who have lived in Brazil for twenty or more years, the first of whom went as a missionary priest to the rural interior, the other who went originally as a student to the city of São Paulo.

(I)

When I went down there, I didn't know *what* was going on. Jánio Quadros quit as president shortly after I got there. Then Goulart took over, and he seemed to be a leftist . . . I'm trying to give you an idea of how I felt personally. We knew that the Communists were going to take over. That was not an idle threat. Their propaganda was very explicit and very open. Even in the convent school where I was teaching there was this publication by a French Dominican. It was all anti-American propaganda. . . . We had visions that we were going to be thrown out, destroying the whole mission that we had built up for years.

(II)

I received a Fullbright to study for two years at the University of São Paulo. While I was there, Catholic

Action was really in its heyday. This was around
1958, 59, 60, 61, 62, 63 — until 64, really was a
completely different kind of situation — one of the
most open political situations I had ever seen in my
life. So much hope. . . . There were many Dominican priests who were chaplains to Catholic Action
groups. . . . All of this time I was working with
different Church programs — social programs, political programs — until the revolution of 1964 (i.e.,
the military coup), which made all of that very, very
difficult.

It is interesting to note particular differences between these
two speakers (who are both committed Catholics of approximately the same age and similar social backgrounds). Although
both mentioned the Dominican priests, one seemed to perceive
them as progressive in the positive sense of the term, while
the other presented them as dangerous propagandists. Although both were involved in Church-related work, one perceived the military coup as putting an end to that work, while
the other thought that that would be done by a Communist
revolution. These two persons represented not only differences
in experience and in environment (that is, rural interior and
urban university), but also opposite ends of a whole range of
Church responses to the context of the popular movements in
the early 1960's. Those movements made visible the conflict
and inequality present in the political-economic structure of
Brazil. The variety of Catholic responses to the popular mobilization would also bring to a head certain conflicts within the
Church itself.

NOTES

[1]Emmanuel DeKadt, *Catholic Radicals in Brazil* (London: Oxford University
Press, 1970), pp. 45-46.

[2] As mentioned in Chapter Four, Goulart had entered a presidency greatly weakened by an act of the national legislative assembly. However, within fifteen months, he managed to regain full presidential power by means of a popular vote. This intensified the sense of the power of the popular masses.

[3] Carlos Estevam Martins, "História do CPC" (Photocopied article, source unknown), p. 60.

[4] Thomas E. Skidmore, *Politics in Brazil, 1930-1964: An Experiment in Democracy* (New York: Oxford University Press, 1967), p. 228

[5] Kenneth Paul Erickson, *The Brazilian Corporative State and Working-Class Politics* (Berkeley: University of California Press), p. 131. This section and the next ("The Military") draws mainly from Erickson, as well as from John Humphrey, *Capitalist Control and Workers' Struggle in the Brazilian Auto Industry* (Princeton, N.J.: Princeton University Press, 1982) and Thomas E. Skidmore, *op. cit.*

[6] Octavio Ianni, *Crisis in Brazil* (New York: Columbia University Press, 1970), p. 96.

[7] Erickson, *op. cit.*, p. 131.

[8] Ianni, *op. cit.*, pp. 107-108.

[9] For an explanation of the Paulo Freire method see Freire's own book, *Pedagogy of the Oppressed* (New York: Seabury, 1970).

[10] Movimento de Cultura Popular (MCP), "O Que é o MCP?" (Photocopied article, source unknown), pp. 67-71.

[11] Carlos Estevam Martins, *op. cit.*, pp. 80-82.

[12] *Ibid.*, pp. 77-78.

7
THE CONFLICT
ENTERS THE CHURCH

During a period of rapid social change, the unequal structures of a society may become exposed, helping to generate an increase in critical social consciousness among large segments of the population. Such consciousness often results in the development of popular movements, which exert pressure for greater political participation and for economic equality. There may also be repercussions of popular movements within religious bodies. This happens because religious bodies themselves contain unequal power structures and ideological differences, which provide potential sources of conflict. In Brazil, such conflict was evident in the Catholic Church by 1961, although its seeds had been planted several years earlier in the Catholic Action movement.

I. Catholic Action

The conflict within the Church, which would occur between conservative members of the hierarchy and radical members of JUC (University Catholic Action), was not immediately visible. During the 1950's, JUCists seemed to be simply trying to concretize their Christian commitment in relation to the lived experience of a rapidly changing social context.

It was in 1954 that JUC in Brazil began to make
qualitative changes in its program. In that year, it
adopted as its national theme the social question.
. . . People began to become conscious of social
problems. And so JUC began to define programs according to the living of the reality. And thus began
political participation in general, taking a stronger
presence in real life. I lived through this moment.
                    (A former officer of JUC in São Paulo)

An examination of the themes of the national meetings of
JUC between 1951 and 1960[1] clearly shows the development
to which the above speaker was referring. The 1951 meeting
produced a text for the orientation of JUC teams nationwide.
It was essentially an introspective document. The 1952 meeting
was concerned with the demands of university life and with
the religious formation of the student. In 1953 the concern was
with perfecting the see-judge-act method. Then the 1954 meeting produced a document entitled "The Student and the Social
Question." As though this step were a bit frightening and producing of uncertainty among the militants, the theme of the
1955 meeting seemed to indicate a certain pulling back into
private life — human love and the family. The following year,
however, the students' social milieu once again demanded their
attention, in the form of an inquiry into Brazilian colleges.
Social concerns continued to dominate the two national meetings held in 1957. In connection with the 1959 meeting, Father
Almery Bezerra, chaplain for JUC in Pernambuco, wrote a
report entitled "On the Necessity of a Historical Ideal"[2] that
clearly linked faith to social action. But it was the Tenth-Year
Congress of 1960 that would place JUC on an irreversible path
toward concrete involvement in the transformation of political-
economic structures. At that meeting, the students from the
center-west region presented "Some Directives of a Christian
Historical Ideal for the Brazilian People," a document which

drew from the writings of Thomas Aquinas, Pope Pius XII, Louis Joseph Lebret, Jacques Maritain and Emmanuel Mounier, and which placed the blame for underdevelopment on imperialist capitalism. It proposed, among other things, the abolition of the private ownership of the means of production, the construction of a planned economy, the use of local forces of production for the well-being of the Brazilian people, a reform of the electoral system and egalitarian relations among nations.

If the new consciousness of the Catholic Action militants represented the reverberation of popular movements within the Church, this document would send shock waves back into the larger society. The right-wing press and the conservative politicians immediately noted the leaning toward Marxism that now seemed apparent in JUC, and both clergy and laity began to question this new orientation. The controversy was reflected in articles that appeared in the *Brazilian Ecclesiastical Review* in the early 1960's. Both essays and news items expressed repeatedly the danger of Communism and the importance of the religious mission of Catholic Action. Other articles defended the social engagement of the JUCists. The controversy was intensified by the visit to Brazil of the French Dominican Thomas Cardonnel. Frei Cardonnel spent several months in various parts of the country, encouraging the students along their new path, and, in a series of articles for their journal, furnished them with ideological ammunition, particularly the concepts of "established disorder" and of the violence inherent in unequal social structures. In addition, the Brazilian Jesuit philosopher, Henrique C. de Lima Vaz, helped the JUCists to transform Maritain's concept of the "historical ideal" into the more Marxian "historical consciousness."[3]

The spark that would finally set off the explosion within the Church was the translation of ideology into concrete action. When the JUCists began to try to apply their Christian social commitment, the UNE seemed the logical vehicle. This was not acceptable to the bishops, who saw this action by the students as bringing the Church into politics. It is interesting to note that this objection was being raised within a context where Church-state cooperation was already the norm. However, the students' choice of action had Marxist overtones. As was noted earlier, the government-funded UNE had a strong representation of Communist students in both local and national elected positions.

> We were supposed to be "fighting Communism." But as we began to participate more in student politics, we began to see that the Communists were right about some things, and we began to defend some of those same things. . . . JUCists began using terminology that sounded Marxist and began criticizing the Church. Reactionary politicians started to call the bishops' attention to those "Communist ideas".
> . . . Then, in 1961, when a militant of JUC became national president of UNE, the bishops got worried because this represented political participation by JUC.
>
> (A former JUCist)

Aldo Arantes, the JUCist from the Catholic University of Rio who became UNE president, was expelled from JUC by Dom Jaime Câmara, Cardinal-Archbishop of Rio and President of the CNBB. Subsequently the bishops decided that no militant holding an elected position in JUC could hold an elected position in UNE. Since UNE was singled out, it seems likely that its ideological position had something to do with the bishops' action. An item in the "Church News" section of the *Brazilian Ecclesiastical Review* in June 1962 presented UNE as an arm of Communism and Aldo Arantes as a traitor who had been bought by the position of UNE president. The article went on to warn against the dangers of Communism and of such enemies of Christianity as Fidel Castro, Che Guevara and Francisco Juliâo. It also mentioned seventeen letters and several telegrams (sources not specified) received by Dom Jaime and several other bishops, warning of the "absolute necessity of combatting UNE, contaminated by Communism," "the Communist infiltration of the student milieu" and the necessity to "stimulate the creation of a national organization of students according to Christian principles." Some of the letters had gone as far as reporting the names of Catholic priests allegedly serving as advisors to the new UNE president.

It was obvious to many JUCists that they had reached the limits of the autonomy of the specialized movements within Catholic Action and that most of the bishops did not agree with their view of their right to determine the appropriate action to express their Christian commitment.

> JUC began to come into conflict with the hierarchy over the distinction between political action and evangelizing action. The bishops believed that Catholic Action was supposed to be the extension of the arm of the hierarchy, mandated by the hierarchy.
> (A former JUCist from São Paulo)

There was no real resolution of the conflict, although there were consequences of it. The first was the formation of the Popular Action movement[5] in 1962. A later consequence was the disassociation of JUC from the hierarchy. The bishops had tried increasingly to place stronger controls on JUC.[6] Only a very small group of bishops, which included Dom José Delgado, Dom Cándido Padin, Dom José Távora and Dom Hélder Câmara, defended the young militants. By 1965, the country was under a military dictatorship, and the progressive bishops no longer had the most influential voices in the CNBB. It was in this political and religious context that the hierarchy reorganized Catholic Action in order to return it to the pre-1950 form, in which the lay organizations were under the direct control of the local bishop. The following year, at the annual meeting of JUC, the students declared their organization to be independent of the control of the hierarchy.

> At the meeting of the Central Committee of the CNBB, held on November 8, 9 and 10, the bishops received an official communication from two movements of Brazilian Catholic Action, JUC and JIC, by which they discontinued their participation in Catholic Action and became Christian movements without the particular dependence on the Hierarchy characteristic of Catholic Action. . . . The decision taken by these movements does not signify, in any way, any kind of break with the Hierarchy but is the result of new needs, which many groups of Christians feel at the present time, to give their movements the characteristics demanded by the pluralistic reality of the modern world and by the condition of the "Church in the world."[7]

The response of the CNBB, as expressed by Dom Vicente Scherer, national secretary for lay affairs, was officially to dissolve JUC. The lay militants continued their movement without the approval of the hierarchy for a few years, until it died out in the late 1960's.[8]

II. The Popular Action Movement (AP)

Popular Action was one of the most striking examples of the active influence of religion in relation to social activism, al-

though this influence was not direct. AP was begun mainly by
JUCists (although some non-religious leftists also joined), and
it grew precisely through Catholic Action channels. The origin
of the movement seems to have derived from the growing conflict between the militants and the hierarchy.

> So out of this conflict was born *Ação Popular,* in
> order to provide a vehicle through which Catholic
> militants could act politically. At that time we com-
> bined ideas of Christian humanism, personalism and
> socialism.
>   (A former militant in JUC and AP)

AP's base document included a critique of capitalism, the
Marxism conceptions of history and consciousness and an emphasis on the mobilization of the dominated classes through
conscientization. The document clearly stated that:

> AP thus opts basically for a policy of revolutionary
> preparation, consisting of a mobilization of the
> people, on the basis of the development of their levels
> of consciousness and organization, and strengthen-
> ing this mobilization in a struggle against the dual
> domination that is capitalist (international and na-
> tional) and feudal. . . It is taking on the task of
> elaborating, with the people, on the basis of their
> contribution, the new society.[9]

The position of the hierarchy with regard to AP was openly
critical. The presence of Catholics in AP was seen as the formation of an alliance with Communism and hence with the
enemies of Christian ideals.

AP was founded in 1962 and repressed by the military regime
in 1964. During the two years of its legal existence, certain

factors contributed to its rapid growth:

(1) it drew on the membership of nationwide organizations, primarily JUC and JEC;

(2) it possessed an ideology that justified and advocated the political involvement of Christians in the process of the socialist transformation of Brazilian society;

(3) it was present in several classes and sectors, including students, some labor leadership, professionals, bank clerks and teachers.[10]

It appears that AP's impact on Brazilian society was quite strong. Although it never had more than two or three thousand members, the actual range of its influence was much broader. It reached people who, although they were not official members (and hence were impossible to enumerate), cooperated with the lines of action that were proposed by the AP leadership.[11]

After the coup, AP militants were violently persecuted (as were JUCists because of the overlap between the two organizations), and the movement went underground.

> *Acão Popular* was very active in our area all the way through the repression. They were some of the most valiant workers. Now they had a "heavy" political orientation. In our area they worked very well. I respected them. They had to be very careful. You never knew whether some of them were still alive, because they would disappear.
>
> (A missionary sister)

Eventually AP evolved from a humanistic revolutionary group with vaguely defined beliefs to an underground Maoist organization of urban guerrillas before dying out in the midst of the severe repression of the late 1960's. However, along with JUC, AP left its mark on Church and society.

III. Consequences of AP and JUC for Brazilian Society and for the Catholic Church

The impact of AP was probably more significant before the coup of 1964 than afterwards. It was a vital element in the "Brazilian Revolution." AP influenced thousands of people who committed themselves to mobilization for radical social change by means of a peasant-worker-student alliance and of education for liberation. Many AP people worked in the Basic Education Movement (MEB), which had a lasting effect in the form of rural unions and cooperatives.

In terms of religion, AP seems to have functioned almost in the traditional pattern of a heresy — that is, it was virtually condemned by Church authorities, persecuted by the state and yet still had a subtle but lasting influence on religious belief. It is important to keep in mind that a great many AP members remained active in JUC, which gave them a legitimized voice in the Church until 1966. Thus these AP/JUCists could continue to exercise a prophetic challenge within Brazilian Catholicism by continuing to expose the structural bases of social injustice and the complicity of the Church in a political-economic system characterized by extremes of wealth and poverty. Their involvement in the Basic Education Movement, which was mentioned above in relation to their influence in society, was also relevant to their influence in the Church. MEB was a Church organization and represented an important part of the Church's official response to social problems. It thus had an influence on the way many lay people, nuns, priests and bishops defined the relationship of faith to action in the secular sphere. This meant the development of a belief system in which spirituality and social action were defined as unified and in which the preferential option for the poor would be a central element. Thus indirectly, through JUC and MEB, AP influenced the development of the option for the poor.

Since the relationship between JUC and AP was one of overlap but not of total identity, it is important to specify the influence of JUC itself on the Brazilian Catholic Church. What is said about JUC should also be applied to JEC.

> The importance of JEC is not usually noted, because its consequences most often became evident after its militants had "graduated" to JUC . . . Many AP people started out in JEC. Many members of JEC became priests and sisters, including the most progressive leadership in the religious orders of women in Brazil today. JEC played a fundamental role in preparing leadership at all levels of the Church. Many of the most forward looking bishops had been chaplains in JUC and JEC. One of the influences of JEC was the spirituality of poverty — that is, the belief that it is among the poor that the reign of God can be realized. In 1961 JECists were already talking about the option for the poor.
>
> (A religious sister and former member of JUC and JEC)

> The majority of the professors at the Regional Seminary in Olinda were also chaplains in JEC, JUC and JOC, in descending numerical order. This particular seminary had a reputation for being progressive with regard to social issues. In the 1960's, there was an increase in the amount of social sciences in the curriculum, more political economy and even some Marxism. This particular seminary prepared priests for a fairly large region (in the Northeast), and these younger priests were in sympathy with the popular movements.
>
> (A former seminarian and JOCist from Pernambuco)

Thus it appears that Catholic Action, particularly JEC and JUC, influenced the Church through the early spiritual formation of lay activists, some of whom became sisters and priests, as well as through those chaplains who became seminary professors and bishops. It seems ironic that the militant lay movements would leave their mark on Brazilian Church history through non-lay persons. Since military repression would thwart the efforts of lay activists, the most lasting influence of Catholic Action would be through the hierarchy.[12]

In terms of the preferential option for the poor, Catholic Action influenced three major areas of religious belief — the role of the laity, critical social consciousness and the communitarian dimension of faith.

Catholic Action linked the official Church to sectors of the laity and to the changing social environment. Although the question of the full extent of lay responsibility that surfaced in the conflict between JUC and the CNBB led to the demise of Catholic Action, the path had been prepared for a partial democratization of clergy-laity relations. There would be a validation of the role of the laity as agents both of evangelization and of social transformation.

> Catholic Action woke up the lay people. It generated the participation of the laity in the life of the Church, in the task of evangelization and in discussing Christianity relative to the problems of the world.
> . . . Catholic Action produced an opening for the lay people. There was a mutual influence between the priest and the lay persons.
> (A former JEC/JUCist from Pernambuco)

> If there had not been the experience of Catholic Action, the role of the lay people would not have been given value.
> (A former JUC state officer from São Paulo)

Another consequence of Catholic Action was to awaken the Church in Brazil to the social-historical dimension of faith. The see-judge-act method provided a means of dealing with a changing social reality, calling attention to the injustices in the political-economic structure and changing the Church's orientation toward the poor from assistentialism to conscientization.

> The important influence of Catholic Action was awakening the Church to the social dimension of faith — not purely (political) ideology but faith. Unlike Marxism, the social criticism came from the Word of God.
> (Dom Marcelo Cavalheira, Bishop of Guarabira and former rector of the Regional Seminary in Olinda)

> See, judge, act — what is it that one sees? In countries with a less visibly conflictive social reality, the problems which militants discussed were more likely to be personal ones. But when we looked at the Brazilian reality, we saw one full of conflict.
> (A former national officer of JEC)

> The Church began to develop a social consciousness and to turn toward the rural poor and the factory workers. . . . Catholic Action played an important role in this process of opening within the Church.
> (A former seminarian and MEB staff member)

Catholic Action also helped to prepare the movement of the Church toward the basic ecclesial communities. The reflection on the role of laity and on the social reality were part of this process. In addition, Catholic Action helped generate experiences that would be important in the basic communities — those of communitarian faith, of working with people in their own milieux and of mutual education between lay people and pastoral agents.

> Catholic Action inspired many things. It worked with people in their milieu. In certain ways, it was a preparation for those movements of today. . . . Another insight is the apostolate of the laity in their own milieu — that the ones being educated may also be the educators. To the extent that this insight was assimilated [into the Church], it had an influence on the basic ecclesial communities.
>
> (Dom José Lamartine Soares, Auxiliary Bishop of Olinda/Recife)

Finally, through former chaplains, such as Dom Hélder Câmara, Catholic Action as it developed in Brazil influenced the Emergency Plan of the CNBB (1962), the Second Vatican Council (1963-1965) and the meeting of the Latin American bishops at Medellín (1968).

> The Emergency Plan was the work primarily of Dom Hélder Câmara, who at the time was the Secretary General of the CNBB.
>
> (Francisco Whitaker — one of the writers of the Unified Pastoral Plan)

> I just keep going back to [the subject of] Dom Hélder Câmara, because he was at the core of it. When the bishops were meeting at Medellín, that was really one of the first times they came to grips with the situation and said, "There's an injustice, and the Church has to face it." It's just a super document. But what I understand is that when they gathered and set up the commission to put the Medellín Docu-

ments together, Dom Hélder had "infiltrated" and had his own theologians in there. And so what you have here, with Medellín, is a Dom Hélder Câmara document.

(A missionary priest)

Meanwhile, the Vatican Council was moving along, and when *Gaudium et Spes* came out, we said [laughing], "They're copying what we're doing here!" We would look at *Gaudium et Spes* and say, "This part here comes from Dom Hélder!"

(Monseignor Expedito Sobral de Medeiros, Pastor of São Paulo do Potengí)

God prepared the Second Vatican Council by means of several movements: The Biblical movement, the liturgical movement and Catholic Action, with its emphasis on the position of the laity in the Church and the specific domain of the laity as a Christian presence in the world.

(Dom Hélder Câmara)

Catholic Action would be like the seed that dies while the plant takes root. Restricted by the hierarchy, persecuted by the military regime and later disowned by Catholic radicals under the charge of being elitist, the specialized movements were nonetheless a critical factor in the development of the preferential option for the poor.

NOTES

[1]Márcio Moreira Alves, *A Igreja e a Política no Brasil* (São Paulo: Editora Brasiliense, 1979), pp. 124-125.

[2]Reprinted in Luiz Gonzaga de Souza Lima, *Evolucão Politica dos Católicos e da Igreja no Brasil*. (Petrópolis Vozes, 1979), pp. 79-83, as is the next document cited.

[3]Historical consciousness refers to the awareness by the proletariat of their role in the overthrow of capitalist society. The replacement of a concept of Maritain by one of Marx must have been alarming to those bishops who feared the Communist infiltration of the Catholic student movement.

[4]*Brazilian Ecclesiastical Review (Revista Eclesiástica Brasileira)* 22, 2 (1962), pp. 496-498.

[5]AP will be discussed in Section II of this chapter.

[6]Among the bishops' attempts to control JUC were the expulsion of Aldo Arantes from JUC when he became president of UNE, the ruling made that no JUCist could simultaneously hold office in both JUC and UNE and the reorganization of Catholic Action from a national body with a lay directorate to diocesan groups directly controlled by their individual bishops.

[7]*Brazilian Ecclesiastical Review* 27, 1 (March, 1967), pp. 189-190.

[8]There are numerous theories to explain the decline of Catholic Action (See Thomas C. Bruneau, *The Political Transformation of the Brazilian Catholic Church* (London: Cambridge University Press, 1974), pp. 125-126; Rubem Alves, "A Volta do Sagrado: Os Caminhos da Sociologia da Religião no Brasil" (*Religião e Sociedade* 1), pp. 128-129; Penny Lernoux, *The Cry of the People* (Garden City, N.Y.: Doubleday, 1980), p. 25; Ivo Lesbaupin, "A Igreja Católica e os Movimentos Populares Urbanos" (*Religião e Sociedade* 5: 189-198), p. 190. What is sociologically important to note is a contradiction between theology and experience. Traditional theology taught that Catholic Action was the laity's participation in the work of the bishops, but not in their power (See Ives Congar, *Lay People in the Church*. Westminster, MD: Newman Press, 1965). In practice, however, the militants experienced considerable autonomy from the hierarchy, especially since they had a national organization that freed them from the direct control of the local bishops. Nevertheless, some of the bishops continued to assume that Catholic Action was an extension of the arm of the hierarchy, and was supposed to be fighting Communism. When JUCists began instead to talk like Marxists, the bishops took action to control the movement (see note 6 above) and, failing that, dissolved it.

[9]The complete AP base document is reprinted in Lima, *op. cit.,* pp. 118-144.

[10]Lima, *op. cit.,* pp. 43-44.

[11]Emanuel De Kadt, *Catholic Radicals in Brazil* (London: Oxford University Press, 1970), pp. 82-83.

[12]I have been unable to obtain an exact number defining how many progressive bishops had been Catholic Action chaplains. Interviewees tended to say "a lot of them." One informant, himself a bishop and a former JEC chaplain, simply said that there were "too many to count." Another said that there was a period of time (1960's) when one might have thought that the chief criterion for the appointment of a bishop was experience as a Catholic Action chaplain.

8
THE BRAZILIAN REVOLUTION: MILITARY STYLE

Brazil had a tradition of temporary military interventions,[1] after which the army would always return the government to civilian hands. The military role seemed to be the upholding of the constitution or the restoration of order in the face of chaos. Goulart's administration certainly met the criterion of chaos. His personal behavior did not exactly inspire admiration — from his reputation for corruption to his inclination toward creature comforts. Even more serious were the signs of his weakness as a president — vacillations, inconsistencies and rather clumsy attempts at populist opportunism.[2] But it was his courting of the radical left which proved to be particularly alarming to the landowners, the urban bourgeoisie and the United States government.

> The coup was mainly the product of the large landowners, multinational corporations and United States imperialism. It was justified by the national debt, corruption in the Goulart government and accusations of political subversion.
>
> (A former peasant league organizer)

The revolt of the military officers against the Goulart government began in Minas Gerais on March 31, 1964. Goulart had ordered the First Army, headquartered in Rio, to crush that "insignificant rebellion in Minas."[3] However, when the troops from Minas reached Rio, the president had fled to Brasília, leaving word that he wanted no military clash. Consequently, one sector of the military after another joined the revolt.

On the night of April 1, Goulart left Brasília for his home state of Rio Grande do Sul, on the Uruguayan border, and the President of the Senate declared the presidency vacant. A few days later, Goulart crossed into Uruguay.

Meanwhile the left was caught completely by surprise. Their optimism and revolutionary spirit suddenly dissolved in the face of the harsh new reality. Hundreds of activists were arrested or forced to leave the country. Many radical leaders went underground. The CGT called for a general strike, but it did not happen.

> In 1964 the army just stood up and walked all through Brazil and nobody took one shot.
>
> (A lay pastoral agent)

The military take-over had been easier than anticipated, and this time would not be temporary. There is evidence that the United States embassy had offered assistance in the form of "military materiels," but that this help was not needed.[4] On April 2, President Lyndon Johnson sent good wishes to the new government of Brazil. These wishes were soon followed by increased economic and military aid.[5]

On April 9, the military issued the first Institutional Act, which would give the next president a great deal of power over Congress as well as the power to suppress the political rights of "undesirables" for ten years. The Institutional Act also stipulated that a new president should be elected within two days and cancelled the clause in the Constitution which barred active military officers from the presidency. On April 11, the generals chose the coordinator of the military conspiracy, General Humberto de Alencar Castelo Branco, as the new president.

Among the nearly four hundred people whose political rights were suspended were labor leaders, military officers, intellectuals and public officials. The latter included the three most recent presidents; six state governors, including Miguel Arraes, the progressive governor of Pernambuco; and fifty-five congressmen, including Francisco Julião. Organizations promoting social change were outlawed, including the Peasant Leagues, the General Confederation of Workers, the National Student Union and Popular Action (AP).

Many of the AP militants who were jailed or forced into exile were JUCists. Several Catholic Action chaplains were also targets of repression. This fact, however, did not inspire the majority of the bishops to defend the persecuted priests or lay radicals. In fact, in May 1964, the CNBB had the following to say about the national situation:

> Attentive to the general and anxious hope of the Brazilian people, who saw the accelerated march of Communism for the conquest of power, the Armed Forces stepped in just in time, and prevented the implantation of the Bolshevik regime in our Land . . . In giving thanks to God, who heard the prayers of millions of Brazilians and delivered us from the Communist peril, we thank the Military men, who, with serious risk to their lives, acted in the name of the nation, and we are grateful to all those who came together to liberate it from the imminent abyss.[6]

Later in the text, the bishops did go on to say that they refused to accept the accusations that Catholic Action and the Basic Education Movement were Communist. Apparently this protest was not strong enough for the militants.

> In '64 there were more Catholic Actionists arrested than there were Communists or anything else. In 1968 it was even worse. Many of the leaders were exiled. They were furious with the official Church.
>
> (A lay pastoral agent)

At this point in time, there were probably no fewer progressive bishops and priests than there had been before the coup. However, there was a shift of power within the hierarchy that would change the location of the progressives and the vehicles through which they would work. Dom Eugênio Sales, who was accused in the national legislative assembly of being a Communist, was made archbishop of Salvador da Bahia, an appointment which removed him from the then-controversial archdiocese of Natal (and Dom Eugênio himself began to move more toward the right). Dom Hélder Câmara, an auxiliary bishop in Rio de Janeiro and Secretary General of the CNBB, was made archbishop of Olinda and Recife (in the northeast). Then the CNBB elections held in Rome in late 1964 (during the Vatican Council) displaced all the progressive bishops from the top positions in the Conference. These positions would subsequently be held by bishops who had had no previous experience in the CNBB and no commitment to social change.[7] This meant that more traditional bishops would have the upper hand in the Church in Brazil during the very same period when world Catholicism, in the midst of the Vatican Council, was becoming more open to renewal. However, the seeds of change had been planted, and the Brazilian Catholic Church would not be able to return to its old alliances with economic and military elites.

NOTES

[1]Relatively recent examples of temporary military interventions are the coup that brought the civilian dictatorship of Getúlio Vargas to power in 1938 and the "preventive coup" of 1955 which guaranteed the presidential inauguration of Juscelino Kubitschek after his legal election in the face of threats of a coup against him (see Skidmore, *op. cit.*, pp. 154-158).

[2]Skidmore, *op. cit.*, pp. 262-263, 283-284. Much of the background information for this chapter is from Skidmore.

[3]Skidmore, *op. cit.*, p. 301.

[4]Skidmore quotes from an account in the newspaper *O Estado de São Paulo*, describing one of three contacts between the military conspirators and the United States Embassy shortly before March 31, 1964:

> "A high (Brazilian) official was asked about the possibility of meeting with one of the members of the military section of the Embassy of the United States. He agreed to hold a conversation at the office of the latter. The meeting took place, and on that occasion he received, couched in diplomatic language, an offer of war materiels in case of necessity. His response was one of sincere thanks and it was accompanied by the following explanation: 'Brazil, sir is a country different from all others. In the decisive moment, I am certain that we here, with our own forces, will know how to resolve the situation. Arms we do not need. We have enough for an action, even if it is a long one. But I admit that we may face the need for fuel, and in that case perhaps I will contact you.' "

(Skidmore goes on to say:)

> The fact is that this assistance (never, according to his account, actually promised — its availability was deduced from an "impression") was never needed, and therefore the American authorities could afterward state unequivocally that they had not assisted the rebels. That their sympathy lay with the conspiracy seems undeniable.

> After the overthrow of Goulart, the American government made clear that it was delighted with the turn in Brazilian politics. Within hours after President Ranieri Mazilli had been sworn in as the Acting President of Brazil in the early morning hours of April 2, President Lyndon Johnson sent a message expressing "warmest good wishes" and stating that "the American people have watched with anxiety the political and economic difficulties

through which your great nation has been passing, and have admired the resolute will of the Brazilian community to resolve these difficulties within a framework of constitutional democracy and without civil strife." [A footnote here cites the *New York Times,* April 3, 1964.] The surprising rapidity of the American recognition of Goulart's overthrow helped to reinforce the suspicion that the United States had played some role in the Brazilian coup.

(Skidmore, *op. cit.,* pp. 326-327)

⁵Skidmore, *op. cit.,* pp. 327, 329.

⁶Reprinted in Lima, *op. cit.,* p. 147.

⁷Bruneau, *op. cit.,* p. 124.

9
THE SEEDS BEGIN
TO TAKE ROOT

I. A Period of Latency?

At the time of the coup, the Church appeared to be relatively silent with regard to social and political issues. With conservatives in key positions in the CNBB, the prophets did not have a voice, as they had had earlier and would have again within a decade.

In order to understand what might have appeared as a backward step in the Church's ideological position, it is important to consider the total historical context. It would seem plausible that the presence of political repression may have led to a certain caution on the part of some of the bishops regarding the taking of explicit positions on political issues. In addition, there was also the sense of relief among many Church people over the end of the chaos of Goulart's presidency. This may have led some of the bishops to be wary of any person or group claiming to represent the left. Finally, there was a certain wait-and-see attitude about the new regime, to allow the generals time to show what their rule would be about.

I think maybe there was some relief. Some people might have felt also a kind of stability when the revolution occurred. But then we realized that it was a revolution that did not represent the people at the bottom of the ladder. The government wanted to keep a lid on things. So if anybody came out and said anything that might in any way agitate the people, they would step on them. People were being denied basic rights. . . . It struck me that, at all costs, the government was going to be in control.

(A missionary priest)

There was certainly a potential for the Church to remain a conservative social force, to support the existing powers and to define charity solely in terms of almsgiving. The Medellín documents did not yet exist in 1964, and the preferential option for the poor was not in widespread use as part of the religious vocabulary. However, there was already a new mechanism in place — unified pastoral planning by the CNBB — that had placed the Church on a virtually irreversible path. The following pages retrace the development of this institutional feature, which began well before the coup.

II. The Pastoral Plans

1. THE EMERGENCY PLAN (PE)

It was Pope John XXIII who helped to institutionalize change in the Brazilian Church. In 1958, Pope John had urged the representatives of the Latin American Bishops Conference meeting in Rome to take action in relation to the critical condition of the Church on their continent. In 1961, in a letter to all the Latin American bishops, the pope repeated his plea with greater urgency, given the increasing speed of historical transformations (possibly referring to the Cuban revolution) and the inadequacy of pastoral renovation. In particular, Pope John urged the setting up of national bishops' conferences, the drawing up of unified pastoral plans by these conferences and the commitment of the bishops to the work of human social betterment (*promoção humana*).[1]

Brazil already had a national bishops' conference (the CNBB had likely been the inspiration for the Pope's suggestion), which lost no time in taking action on the letter. By the middle of 1962, the Emergency Plan was in existence. As was indicated in Chapter Seven, this plan was primarily the work of Dom Hélder Câmara, one of Brazil's most innovative bishops. The linking of Dom Hélder to the Emergency Plan is interesting and important for two reasons:

(1) This suggests an influence on the Emergency Plan that came from a bishop who had allowed himself to be educated by Catholic Action militants on the importance of the contribution of the laity to the Church;

(2) Dom Hélder was also aware of what the bishops of the northeast were doing, in terms of both social programs and pastoral planning.

> Dom Hélder exchanged a lot of ideas with Dom Eugênio even before becoming archbishop of Olinda and Recife. Two or three times a year Dom Eugênio would visit him in Rio and Dom Hélder would come to Natal. . . . Dom Eugênio had influence [on the Emergency Plan]. The main idea of the Emergency Plan came out of the plan for Natal — even right down to the rural unions.
> (Monseignor Expedito Sobral de Medeiros)

The Emergency Plan focused on four areas — renewal of the

clergy, renewal of Catholic education, restructuring of the parishes and social-economic programs. The role of the laity was integrated into the last two areas, both of which are of particular interest in relation to the development of the preferential option for the poor.

Although the Emergency Plan presented the bishop as pastor by divine right, the parish priest was to be the educator of the militant laity, who should be engaged in the reconstruction of the social order according to Christian teaching. The priest should see to it that the laity assumed the initiative and the principal responsibility in this temporal task. A strong emphasis was placed on Catholic Action as a movement which would help to facilitate the goals of the pastoral plan.

> It is necessary that the pastor:
> —trust in the possibilities of the laity
> —raise up militants and leaders in their
>   natural communities
> —try to get to know the psychology of
>   the laity at the present moment.
> [The Catholic Action movements] are the link between the parish community and people engaged in the construction of the temporal order. By means of their militants and their active method, they can reach all environments and all people.[2]

Another important feature of parish renewal that tied in with the active role of the laity and with engagement in the temporal order was parish decentralization, which would later be recognized as the foundation for the basic ecclesial communities. It was suggested that the enormous parishes characteristic of Brazil encompassed smaller "natural communities,"[3] and that these communities should be recognized in parish pastoral planning.

In them we shall initiate the work of renewal, seeking
to form an authentic community of faith, of worship
and of charity.[4]

The Emergency Plan represented the beginning of a new era
for the Brazilian Catholic Church. It gave the official Church
a new dynamic, a new structure and a new field of action. It
prepared the way for co-responsibility[5] among the bishops and
for unified pastoral planning, as well a for a strong role for the
laity and a commitment to social change. It was a first step in
a process of change for the religious institution, a step that
was taken with a certain sense of urgency.

> The Emergency Plan was the first step, in response
> to the directive from Pope John XXIII. It was a plan
> of urgency. . . . It was urgent to draw up a global
> plan for the whole Church in Brazil.
> (Monseignor Expedito Sobral de Medeiros)

> The very fact that they called it an emergency plan
> means that they were quite concerned. That *Plano
> de Emergência* was trying to form a community of
> faith and of love. . . . It was trying to bring about
> a renovation, a renewal in the areas of evangelization
> and catechetics, deepening the faith.
> (A missionary priest)

The Emergency Plan was intended as a temporary measure,
to be replaced by a more carefully worked out Unified Pastoral
Plan within three years. However, in itself, the Emergency
Plan was important for the following reasons:

(1) it gave immediate legitimation to priests and lay persons
whose work was oriented toward the preferential option for the
poor;

(2) it made suggestions[6] that would later be implemented in the form of basic ecclesial communities.

(3) it provided for the establishment of CERIS (Center for Religious Statistics and Social Research), an organization which would supply information to be used systematically in further pastoral planning.

2. THE UNIFIED PASTORAL PLAN (PPC)

The Unified Pastoral Plan (*Plano de Pastoral de Conjunto,* or "PPC") was similar in goal to the Emergency Plan — that is, the revitalization of the Church in the face of modernization — but it differed both in its means of formulation and in the social context in which it was written.

The Emergency Plan had been adopted before the coup, when Communism was still perceived as a threat to the Church's mission of salvation. The Unified Pastoral Plan, on the other hand, represented the institutionalization[7] of the preferential option for the poor *after* the coup, when the threat from the left no longer existed. It is clear from the Emergency Plan that concern about Communism was an important stimulus, both for the plan itself and for the letter from Pope John that had called it forth. In Brazil after 1964, that concern had been virtually eliminated, but a new institutional process had already been set in motion. The influence of progressive Brazilian bishops on the climate of renewal at the Vatican was returning home in the spirit of the Council. So Church renewal was becoming not merely a defensive reaction to an external stimulus, but rather an internal dynamic perceived as having its own intrinsic merit and its inspiration from the Holy Spirit. Thus the preferential option for the poor was becoming an integral part of religious belief in the Brazilian Catholic Church and, as an established institutional element, would have the potential for an active social role. In the new context of an authoritarian military regime, this element of religious belief would become a source of critical social analysis and public protest.[8]

It is not likely that most of the bishops who approved the Unified Pastoral Plan were aware of its revolutionary potential, particularly since the CNBB by 1965 had a relatively conservative leadership. Rather the bishops were responding to religious directives from Rome and praying for guidance from the Holy Spirit.

In addition to the social context, it is also important to note the particular method of formulation of the Unified Pastoral Plan. This time the writer of the plan was not a bishop. The PPC was written by a priest-theologian and a layman, with additional input from a priest-sociologist. The theologian was Father Raimundo Caramuru de Barros, a former JAC chaplain who had also worked closely with Dom Hélder Câmara at the time that the latter was writing the Emergency Plan. The sociologist was Father Afonso Gregory of CERIS. The layman was Francisco Whitaker, a former JUC state president in São Paulo and a specialist in social planning who had worked with Father Lebret in Economy and Humanism.[9]

> The Emergency Plan had been a collection of directives, of orientations. The Unified Pastoral Plan was on another level. It was an attempt to be more systematic, by means of the more precise methodology of planning. It involved a long process of discussion all over the country of the methodology of the plan.
> . . All of our meetings had a well-developed theological element, because the purpose of the document would be to understand the implications of Vatican II for pastoral action. . . . The CNBB asked me to help with the adaptation of the technique of planning (to pastoral action), and it was in that capacity that

I participated for two years in the preparation of the plan.

(Francisco Whitaker)

In reflecting on the process described in this quote, one may take note of certain points with regard to the manner in which the PPC was prepared:

(1) it combined input from theology and social science, particularly the techniques of social planning;

(2) it involved a two-year process, with input sought from all regions of the country; there was a conspicuous attempt to solicit the participation of a large number of people, in contrast to the imposition "from the top down" of a plan devised by either clerical or lay elites;

(3) one of the main writers of the plan was a layman, whose own personal formation had included very active participation in JUC during the 1950's — the very time period when JUCists were developing their social-political commitment. This fact is significant in relation to the growing institutional role of lay people in the Brazilian Church, as well as evidence of the continued influence of specialized Catholic Action, in spite of the conflict between JUC and the hierarchy going on at that very time.

The objectives of the PPC were stated in both general and specific terms. The general objectives were stated as follows:

To create milieux and conditions so that the Church in Brazil will adjust, as rapidly and as completely as possible, to the image of the Church of Vatican II. . . . To bring all men [sic] into full communion of life with the Father and between them, in Jesus Christ, in the gift of the Holy Spirit, by means of the visible mediation of the Church.[10]

There were six specific objectives:

(1) to renovate and dynamize the Church in its own ministry of community, strengthening its visible unity;

(2) to bring people to a primary personal commitment to Christ, by means of the missionary announcing of the Word and the witness of evangelical life;

(3) to bring the People of God to a greater communion of life in Christ, by means of Scripture;

(4) to bring the People of God to a greater communion of life in Christ, by means of the renewal of the liturgy;

(5) to bring the People of God to a greater communion of life in Christ, by means of ecumenical action;

(6) to bring the People of God to a greater communion of life in Christ, by means of their insertion as a ferment in the reconstruction of the world according to the plans of God.[11]

These goals are clearly religious. More specifically, they are spiritual, evangelical and ecclesial. Furthermore, although one of the writers of the plan was an active Catholic layman with a strong commitment to social change, most of the bishops who would approve and implement the PPC had more traditional concerns — that is, the salvation of the faithful and the implementation of an effective means for the chruch to have an active influence in a changing society. At the same time that the Brazilian reality was demanding that the Church adapt if it would survive in the modern world, the Second Vatican Council was encouraging the same.

From a sociological viewpoint, there is nothing particularly unexpected about Vatican II or the Unified Pastoral Plan. They are both manifestations of the Church's historical capacity for adaptation and survival. That capacity was updated by the CNBB through the use of social research to inform its pastoral decisions. In any case, the actions of most of the Brazilian bishops in the mid-1960's were essentially conservative in their initial motivation. *However* — and this is a point missed by those social scientists who restrict their view of the Chruch to the self-preservation model[12] — whatever were the original motives of the more traditional bishops, the consequences of their conservative actions would eventually prove to be revolutionary, in the sense of presenting a challenge to both religious and secular power structures. The key to those revolutionary consequences was the openness to input from the laity. In Brazil, as in Latin America as a whole, the majority of the lay people are from the poorer classes, and increasing numbers of these people are becoming conscious that their oppression is not the will of God but rather the result of the extreme inequality present in humanly created social structures. By opening the Church to input from the laity, the bishops were opening it to the preferential option for the poor.

To understand why conservative bishops would do such a thing, one must examine the demands of the previous Emergency Plan in relation to the practical problem of staffing. An important element of the PE, and of the pastoral experiments (such as the Natal Movement) that had formed part of its inspiration, was parish decentralization. This was necessitated by the fact that the large parish structures were unable to compete with other influences (such as Protestantism, spiritism and socialism). However, given Brazil's historical shortage of clergy, this decentralization could not be accomplished without help from another ecclesial sector — the lay people. To survive, the Church was forced to give voice to those members of the hierarchy (such as Dom Hélder and other former Catholic Action chaplains) who advocated a strong ecclesial role for the laity.

In a Church traditionally ruled by bishops, this represents a slight shift in the religious power structure, although *not* a

dismantling of magisterial authority. The ultimate authority
of the bishops was clearly stated in the Unified Pastoral Plan:

> The bishops govern their own churches, through
> trust, counsel, exhortations and examples, but also
> with authority and sacred power . . .

> The bishop, in his diocese, is the authentically
> guaranteed presence of the apostolic succession and
> mission, the center of unity of the people of God,
> entrusted with their guidance, the link in their con-
> nection with the universal Church.

> The initiative (for Church renewal) need not neces-
> sarily come from him, but it requires his own consent,
> manifested and effective.[13]

The role of the laity as articulated in the Unified Pastoral
Plan is similar to what was presented in the Emergency Plan
and in the documents of Vatican II and to what had been developed in specialized Catholic Action — that is, the active
presence of the Church in the temporal order.

> The laity exercise their part in the mission of the
> whole Christian people in the Church and in the
> world. This secular character is particular to the
> laity. Their specific vocation is to search for the King-
> dom of God in the exercising and ordering of temporal
> functions according to God. Theirs is the task of il-
> luminating and ordering in such a manner all tem-
> poral things, to which they are intimately united, to
> make them grow according to Christ.[14]

The decision to trust the lay people in temporal matters would
translate, in the Brazilian social context, to listening to the
poor in both pastoral and political matters. The latter alone

would have provided a potential for religious belief to play a revolutionary part in social conflict. However, the Church could not advocate a restructuring of the temporal order while itself remaining completely within the medieval structure of authority. Although the Unified Pastoral Plan retained the ultimate religious power (that is, the magisterium) for the bishops, it opened the way for some collegiality of the bishops with the priests, religious sisters and brothers and lay people. This is particularly evident in the system of diocesan pastoral planning advocated by the plan:

> The diocesan assembly [should be] formed by all the priests involved in pastoral ministry, by representatives of religious communities, by diocesan directorates of lay movements and institutions, by lay people who perform a task of coordination on the diocesan level (catechetics, liturgy, etc.). The function of this assembly is not only consultative. Through it the whole people of God participates in the life of the diocese and in dialogue with the bishop. . . . This council should include clergy, religious and lay people.[15]

In addition to input on social and pastoral matters, the Unified Pastoral Plan recognized the possibility of a specifically spiritual function for lay people under certain circumstances (presumably the scarcity of priests would strongly affect those circumstances). This would open the way for a diversity of lay ministries, including auxiliary sacramental roles.

> Also the laity can, in many ways, be called to a cooperation that is more immediate with the apostolate of the hierarchy. They may be designated by the hierarchy for some ecclesiastical functions with a spiritual goal.[16]

It is important to note that the lay ministries were to be designated according to the judgment of the bishops. Nevertheless the practical necessity to trust the laity in religious roles could eventually provide a potential for the gradual democratization of religious power.

The Unified Pastoral Plan did not require the compliance of all the bishops. In fact, it reinforced the authority of each bishop over his diocese. Nevertheless, both the general spirit of the plan and its specific recommendations would provide encouragement and legitimation to priests, sisters and lay people who were trying to bring about innnovations within the Church. One of the most important recommendations of the Unified Pastoral Plan was the basic ecclesial community.

III. The CEBs: A Quiet Continuation of Conscientization

The basic ecclesial communities were only hinted at in the Emergency Plan. The Unified Pastoral Plan, however, explicitly recommended their formation:

> Parish decentralization is urgently needed not necessarily in the sense of creating new parishes, but rather of raising up and dynamizing, within the parish territory, base communities (such as rural chapels) where Christians are not anonymous persons merely seeking a service or fulfilling an obligation, bur rather feel welcomed and responsible, and form an integral part of (the communities) in a living communion with Christ and with all their brethren.[17]

In every section of pastoral recommendations, there were specific points made in connection with basic communities. It is clear that the CNBB was leading the Brazilian Catholic

Church as a whole toward this new structural form as early as 1965. There does not appear to be any claim that the bishops were inventing the CEBs. The wording of the recommendations would seem to imply that they were giving their encouragement to an innovation that already existed.

Exactly what were these little communities that were destined to play such an important part in the future of the Latin American Catholic Church? They were groups of approximately ten to thirty people who were encouraged to gather together regularly for the discussion of the relationship of Scripture to their personal and collective lives. Out of these groups would come both communitarian and religious dimensions: Mutual aid, sociability, preparation for the sacraments and, in the absence of a priest, the Sunday celebration of the Liturgy of the Word.

To the conservatives among the bishops, the CEBs may have appeared to be providing a solution to certain pastoral problems:

(1) the preservation of the faith in the absence of a sufficient number of priests to deal with new pastoral demands in a rapidly changing society;

(2) the implementation of the active lay role demanded by the Vatican Council at the very time when the bishops were in the process of rejecting the lay initiative coming from JUC.

> The suppression of JUC left an empty space in the Church, a dislocation at the grassroots. So the Church changed its social base. . . . The CEBs began for the purpose of substituting for the priest. But then they acquired their own lay dynamic.
> (Clodovis Boff)

In the midst of the religious and political conflict associated

with JUC in the mid-1960's, the CEBs may have appeared
pious, docile and politically innocent. There is no indication
that any of the bishops had difficulty in accepting them in
principle, although there was a great deal of variation in episcopal zeal in relation to the actual implementation of this and
other recommendations of the pastoral plan. Nevertheless, this
plan *was* termed "unified" — seeming to indicate that it had
been given at least verbal approval by the CNBB for implementation throughout Brazil and that its spirit could be picked up
by nuns, priests and lay people in different parts of the country.
Furthermore, there were vehicles other than dioceses for the
spread of new pastoral forms.

> One of the contributions of Catholic Action was the
> creation of nationwide networks of people. So pas-
> toral agents are not totally influenced by their
> bishops, because they can be in touch with people in
> other parts of Brazil. Also, dioceses with conservative
> bishops can be influenced by basic ecclesial com-
> munities in neighboring dioceses. In this way, CEBs
> may spread from one diocese to another without the
> bishop's being supportive of them.
>   (A Brazilian sister and former JUCist)

The encouragement of the CEBs would be the thread that
would knit the hierarchy to the Church-at-the-grassroots, and
this new tie would hamper the continuation of the Church's
old alliances with dominant classes. In providing a vehicle
through which middle-class lay people, sisters and priests
would be encouraged to work with the oppressed classes, the
hierarchy was sealing the preferential option for the poor.

The potential for religion to become a force for social change
would also be developed in the CEBs. For it was there that the
method of conscientization, which had been developed in grassroots education programs, could quietly continue.

> It was suggested that we use the ideas of Paulo Freire to help create these communities. . . . The idea was that people would get together, read the Bible and discuss it, and try to see what it had to do with their lives. It was to get people to look at their own reality and try to see what were the problems. Then they would look at those problems in the light of the Gospel and try to work out some response.
>
> (A former missionary sister)

It is clear from the above quote that poor people were not arriving at their new consciousness completely unaided. In examining the links of the hierarchy with the Church-emerging-from-the-grassroots, it is important to consider the nuns, priests and middle-class lay Church workers who would help to forge those links.

IV. Pastoral Agents

The experience of poverty does not automatically generate political consciousness. People who live with unrelieved poverty and injustice more commonly utilize the psychological survival mechanisms of fatalism and other-worldly spirituality. Below are some of the initial responses given by a group of rural people who were new to the dynamic of basic communities. The question asked by the religious sister working with the group was, "Why is the situation as it is (i.e., poverty, lack of land, drought, hunger, etc.)?" The responses of the people:

"The will of God."
"Because of our sins."
"Because we have to pray more."
"Suffering is a test of our faith."
"Those who suffer are closer to God."[18]

Within this same group of poor tenant farmers there were others who were longer-term members of CEBs. Their responses were as follows:

> "There is no rain because the rich people are destroying the forests — the drought is caused by the lack of trees."

> "The landowners do not provide the necessary services for the workers."

> "There are two classes — the rich and the poor. The poor are exploited, humiliated, forgotten; the rich create this situation; the landowners care only for themselves."

> "When there are people who try to help the poor, some end up in prison, the others dead."

These very different sets of responses came from people living within the same rural parish, under similar socio-economic conditions and with similar family and religious backgrounds. The major difference between the people who came up with the two kinds of answers seemed to be the length of time that they had spent as members of basic communities that had been organized by a particular religious sister.

Clodovis Boff, a Brazilian priest and sociologist who spends half of his time teaching in a university and the other half working in a poor rural community, has pointed out that, for a basic community to develop into a vehicle of conscientization, the presence of the right type of "pastoral agent" is indispensable.[19] A pastoral agent is the "new kind" of nun, priest or lay person that has been helping to revolutionize the Latin American Catholic Church. Such persons played an unseen role in the generation of the Unified Pastoral Plan, particularly those sections dealing with the CEBs. They were the persons developing this new way of being Church that the bishops would later discover and endow with institutional legitimacy. Who were the agents who played this key role in pastoral renewal?

It is difficult to generalize about this "new breed," because they came from so many different backgrounds. Some had been involved in specialized Catholic Action, either as chaplains or as lay militants, others had not; some were Brazilians, others were missionaries from Europe or North America; some went into pastoral work with clearly formulated radical political views, others developed their critical consciousness in interaction with the lay people of the poorer classes; some had been involved in pastoral work for many years before Vatican II, others came of age with the spirit of the Council. Perhaps the only elements that all of them had in common were that they were mostly persons from non-poor backgrounds who made a preferential option for the poor, and that they had in some way experienced the Brazilian social-religious context of the late 1950's and early 1960's, a context characterized by a spirit of pastoral innovation and political consciousness. There were several factors that facilitated the development of this spirit:

(1) the experience of Catholic Action;

(2) new approaches in seminaries;

(3) new roles for religious sisters;

(4) a great influx of missionaries and new forms of training for them.

I. The Experience of Catholic Action

Catholic Action influenced pastoral agents by both direct and indirect means. The direct means is obvious. Several persons whom I interviewed in Brazil made reference to former militants who became priests or sisters, as well as bishops and seminary professors who were or had been Catholic Action chaplains.

> [How did the Catholic Action method find its way
> into the basic ecclesial communities?] By way of pas-
> toral agents — bishops, priests and sisters who had
> lived the experience of Catholic Action, whether as
> militants or as advisors. For example, before working
> with basic communities, I was a chaplain for Catholic
> Action.
>
> (Dom Luis Fernandes,
> Bishop of Campina Grande, PB)

The indirect means of influence of Catholic Action is a bit more difficult to specify. It was the general spirit that Catholic Action had helped to generate — a spirit that was characterized by the encouragement of an active lay role and a criticism of social injustice, a spirit that was concretized in the Basic Education Movement, from which it spread throughout the subculture of progressive Catholicism.

> There is also a certain pastoral culture, a certain
> inheritance. The movement of pastoral inspiration
> that animated Catholic Action is also inspiring the
> popular pastoral of today.
>
> (Dom Luis Fernandes)

> Catholic Action influenced the general spirit in the
> Church and thus influenced a lot of people — for
> example, foreign missionaries — who had had no
> contact with Catholic Action themselves.
>
> (Dom Marcelo Cavalheira, Bishop of Guarabira, PB)

2. NEW APPROACHES IN THE SEMINARIES

Interviews and informal conversations with present and former seminarians revealed that there had been a great deal of turmoil and change in the seminaries that began in the early 1960's, and that produced effects which are still being felt at the present time. In addition to curricular innovations, there was a change in the whole way the seminaries were set up.

> There was . . . a mass departure of priests and seminarians in the early 1960's. With so few seminarians remaining, it was not practical to maintain large seminary buildings. Those who remained lived either with their parents or with families at the grassroots. This was an important change. Previously seminarians had been removed from the "real world" during their training. Now they remained in touch with the people. The result was a new type of pastoral work, more in touch with the grassroots.
>
> (A former seminarian)

This change in approach spread to many parts of Brazil and is still evident today. At present there seem to be two types of seminary training: the traditional, separate-from-the-world, academically oriented form and a variety of approaches whose common element seems to be an emphasis on direct pastoral experience among poor people. An example of the latter was described by a religious sister and theology professor who is involved in an alternative program for training seminarians and other pastoral agents:

> To be accepted into our program, the students have to have worked in the popular milieu for at least one year, and they must study without leaving their grassroots work. The students have to understand the reality in which they are living. We ask them to write about their personal motivations, to write a monog-

raph about the social, economic, political, cultural
reality in the community in which they are working
and to keep a diary in which they write about all
aspects of the life of the poor.

Besides describing this training program, this speaker was also
implicitly saying something about herself. The fact that a nun
is involved in teaching future priests, rather than teaching
upper-class young girls in a private school, would seem to
suggest that there have been some drastic changes in the function of religious sisters within the Brazilian Church.[20]

3. NEW ROLES FOR SISTERS

The employment of nuns as pastoral agents has done more
than simply alleviate the Church's personnel problems. There
seems to be a marked difference in the way that priests and
nuns approach the same task, and the feminine input has been
very valuable to the pastoral approach utilized in the basic
communities. I found sisters whom I observed to be consistently
non-directive in their methods of group dynamics and highly
skilled at accompanying,[21] facilitating, drawing people out,
leading people to formulate their own consciousness of their
situation and their own conclusions. The priests, on the other
hand, seemed more inclined to function as preachers, whether
they were preaching the passive acceptance of suffering or Marxist political economy. (Of course, there were notable excep-
tions, but their existence only served to make the general rule
more visible.) These differences may be the result of sex-role
socialization,[22] or of the unequal positions which priests and
nuns have traditionally held within the Church or simply of
the fact that, since women are new to the pastoral role in the
Catholic Church, they do not have to unlearn old patterns.

Following are excerpts from the notes which I took at a variety
of Church gatherings in Brazil, from local community meetings

to large regional assemblies. They illustrate striking examples of the different pastoral styles of women and men.

- I -

(This excerpt is from the same context as the one on pages 109-110.)

One participant questioned the will of God notion. Another suggested that suffering is a test of faith. One of the lay coordinators (whom I later realized had been trained by Sister A.) suggested that God is a father — would a father be so cruel to his children? At this point Father F. spoke up. He said that there is yet another interpretation — God does not allow suffering as a punishment, but rather to strengthen people. Another man questioned this kind of fatherhood. F. then elaborated at great length. (I later learned that A. was struggling with herself as to whether to intervene, sensing that a debate between pastoral agents would not be helpful to the people. She finally decided to do it in the form of a question.) A. asked why, if both the rich and the poor are children of God, they do not all suffer equally. F. replied that there are different kinds of suffering. He went on and on! The lay participants, who had been very active up to this point, suddenly became silent. During the break, A. "huddled" with the lay coordinators. I heard her giving them suggestions as to how to get around F.'s excessive interventions, such as by eliciting responses from various lay people — "and what are *you* thinking, Manoel?" . . . When reports from the small-group discussions were given during the next plenary session, the responses were rather traditional — for example, talking about faith, sacrifice and good works. I suspected that the people were giving the answers that they knew Father F. wanted.

- II -

At certain points during the discussion, a particular priest went on at great lengths with rather intricate political-economic analyses.[23] At some points one of the lay coordinators seemed to be trying to use subtle means to give the discussion back to the lay people. After one of the priest's particularly lengthy discourses, she said something to the effect that, after this excellent but somewhat heavy analysis, it would be good to animate us all with a song. After the song, the priest went right back to his speech. The lay people were becoming quiet. Throughout the day this priest's contribution was quite heavy and frequent. At one point, I overheard a man say that all this material was not going to be of any use back in his community.

- III -

Sister M. presented some materials (which I later learned were related to the history-making meeting of rural and urban union representatives to be held in Saō Paulo in August) in the form of a poster and leaflets. These presented a history of rural and urban unions from the 1920's to the present, with the focus on informing people of what was going on now. C. (a lay person) cracked a joke. M. integrated his joke into her presentation. She presented a second poster, with issues facing the local delegation to the national labor meeting. . . . C. asked several questions. M. stated that she was presenting this information because these struggles would have an effect on the local land movement. People seemed to agree. They contributed both comments and questions. M. further said that she had presented this information for them to do with as they wished, whenever they wished. She repeatedly emphasized that she did not want to put any pressure on them.

Among the priests and sisters whose option for the poor is closely linked with radical political ideology, the goals are similar — to help poor people to arrive at a historical consciousness so that they will struggle to bring about social change. The fact that some pastoral agents use a dialogical approach does not mean that they do not have specific religious and social goals, but rather that they want to help the people to reach their conclusions themselves. In other words, the pastoral agents are not mere facilitators of a process in which they are unconcerned about the outcome. They are deeply concerned. They are people who take seriously the evangelical orientation toward justice, and who are consequently convinced that the present political-economic system has to be changed. It is important to emphasize this point against the widespread ideological assumption that the new form of Church in Brazil is emerging entirely from the poor. The latter are getting a lot of help with the task.

It's not really the people themselves, but rather these [middle-class] people, some of whom would never admit that they are the organizers of what is going on. They would always say that the people organized it, but they (the pastoral agents) really do organize it.

(A lay organizer of basic communities)

This discussion is not intended to imply that the pastoral
agents should not be making a commitment to social justice,
but simply to establish that they do have an important role in
organizing the basic communities and in helping members of
these communities to arrive at a position unifying spirituality
and commitment to social change. The following excerpts from
field notes are intended to illustrate techniques used specifically by sisters in this process. The sisters seemed particularly
inclined to raise questions, ask for summaries, solicit participation by means of concrete and meaningful examples, employ a
variety of animation techniques (including humorous singing
games and puppet shows) and use the phrase, "Please help me
to. . . ."

- I -

A sister coordinated the next session. She asked the
assembly for help in recapping the question from
Thursday morning: What was our motive for coming
here [to the state-wide meeting of CEBs]? Responses
people gave ranged from knowing better the Word
of God to understanding more about CEBs and their
strength. Sister asked whether the presentations of
last night and this morning [songs, poems, dramati-
zations, posters, etc.] had related to those goals.
People replied yes. Then she asked for a recap of the
themes that had emerged from the presentations.
People spontaneously contributed responses: Land-
robbing, unemployment, poor schools, health problems, low wages, the links of the police with the landowners, the lack of roads, the inhumanity of the
mayor, multinational corporations, false hopes and
the lack of organization among the people. Whenever
there was a pause, Sister would say, "What else?"

- II -

At one point during a seemingly endless discussion, M. suddenly started a puppet show at the far end of the hall and recruited C. and T. to join her. The subject of the show, discussed in humorous, high-pitched voices, was "What did you get out of this leadership training week?" The puppet show seemed to have a dual purpose — It woke us all up, and it demonstrated an additional pedagogical technique. M. gave directions on how to make the *papier maché* puppets, and said that the people (whom the community leaders would be organizing) will often talk more freely through puppets.

- III -

At this point in the meeting, A. began to assume a stronger teaching role but did it in a dialoguing way, using vivid examples familiar to the people and asking frequent questions to draw them into the presentation. She began with the observation that one thing had emerged from all the small group reports and asked what that one thing was. A woman responded, "organizing meetings." A. agreed and read off similar responses. She asked questions regarding in what communities things were going very well and why. A couple of people gave specific responses. She asked why people keep on with [CEB] meetings even when "things are weak." Some people responded: Love, will of God, link with God. A. said, "And with whom else?" Someone replied, "With other people." A. built further comments on this last point. . . . then went back to an earlier one: what makes a community

stronger? She used analogies to which people seemed
to relate strongly: several local rural women working
together in the kitchen preparing for a feast day,
and the right combination of ingredients that go into
baking a good cake. She solicited input from everyone
by means of questions. When someone suggested a
parallel to the preparation for the celebration of the
liturgy, A. asked questions about that, too. Then she
started doing a summary by way of questions. When
one man interrupted to relate his own experiences,
she integrated his input also. A.'s total presentation
was fairly long, punctuated by humor and questions
and soliciting participation. She ended by leading
the people in a singing game — with a lot of gestures
— about unity.

Although I observed twenty-five pastoral agents in action
(fifteen of whom were men), the specific techniques described
above were used only by sisters. Among the few priests whom
I did observe using non-directive techniques, their approach
seemed much more low-key. One priest who is very committed
to changing the clerical role sometimes gets his parishioners
to do things for themselves by sitting at meetings with his arms
folded and his mouth shut, to the point that some lay people
have complained about his seeming inactivity. Perhaps this
type of action — or non-action — is precisely what is needed
to break out of the clerical role, particularly when working with
lay people who seem to be trying to preserve that role. Since
sisters, on the other hand, have traditionally played a supportive role in the Church, often in a teaching capacity, it is less
difficult for lay people to accept them in the supportive/
pedagogical role characteristic of the new kind of pastoral
agent.

Whatever the structural or social-psychological reasons, religious women, since the beginning of the Nizia Floresta exper-

iment[24] in the archdiocese of Natal, have played an important role in the development of the basic communities. That their role still remains important seems illustrated by the fact that, whenever I would ask priests or bishops if I might visit CEBs in their areas, they almost always referred me to sisters. In one diocese, however, a bishop referred me to a priest who is considered to be one of the originators of the CEBs. This kind pastor took me to a meeting place only to discover that the meeting had occurred on the previous day. He apologized profusely and explained that the sisters, who were away at the time, would have known the days and times of all the meetings.

4. THE NEW MISSIONARIES

Another important category of pastoral agents are foreign missionaries. In a country as priest-poor as Brazil, there has always been a high proportion of foreign priests and sisters, particularly from Europe.[25] In addition, the number of North Americans increased in the 1960's, as a result of the call from Pope John for missionaries to Latin America.

There were two factors that would predispose these North Americans to utilize new pastoral methods:

(1) since many of the congregations had had no previous mission in Brazil, they had no old roles to unlearn;

(2) in the religious and political environment of the years just before the coup, they would come under the influence of some of the most progressive Church people in Latin America.

When we went down, the first thing we did was to go to CENFI — The Intercultural Formation Center — in Petrópolis. It was like CIDOC [in Cuernavaca, Mexico] and had been founded by Ivan Illich. They had very special people there. The Church in Brazil even then was very forward-looking.

(A former missionary sister)

The Brazilian Church at that time had a very fine group of theologians, sociologists, Church history persons — just a fine group of people who were interested in doing the training of pastoral agents. There was a phase in Brazil when this happened across the country in an amazingly efficient way. Those people became suspect in later periods. It's almost like the Church was euphoric in those years . . until the heavy repression came down on everybody.

(Another missionary sister)

What were the religious and social conditions that facilitated the turning of this motley crew of native and foreign priests and sisters into a large force of pastoral agents who would function as organic intellectuals?[26] The ecclesial reasons were two-fold: the Church needed to innovate in order to survive in the changing social context, and the spirit of Vatican II was further encouraging renewal. The political reason was particularly salient after the coup. The work they were doing was defined as religious and therefore was not immediately the target of repression. So, in 1964, when political work by lay people was crushed, the priests and sisters could quietly continue doing the work of conscientization, because it was part of their religious ministry.

So, in the following years, we tried to learn what the people's agenda was — what the Word of the Lord had to say to them. And so the work became to accompany the people, in the effort to hear them out, to read the story, to read the lives of the people, to read their situation, according to their viewpoint

. . . and to believe that, in their describing of their reality, in their growing awareness of themselves, they would find the answers to the root causes of their problems. . . . I don't mean to say that we had nothing to contribute, but to do that together, mutually, in dialogue, experiencing, to be more a learner than a teacher . . . And so those were the years that what we would come to call "the pedagogical process" became more and more clear.

(A former missionary sister)

These new directions in the Church at the grassroots, facilitated by pastoral agents in the early-to-middle 1960's, would not only develop new structures within the Church. The basic ecclesial communities would also have a special political role to play when the repression became more severe.

NOTES

[1]Raimundo Caramuru de Barros, *Brasil: Uma Igreja em Renovacao* (Petropolis: Vozes, 1968), pp. 25-26.

[2]Conferencia Nacional dos Bispos do Brasil (CNBB), *Plano de Emergência* [Emergency Plan] (Rio de Janeiro: Livraria Dom Bosco Editora, 1962), pp. 17, 20.

[3]An example of a natural community would be a rural village.

[4]Emergency Plan, pp. 22-23.

[5]My reading of the unified Pastoral Plan has been supplemented by reading a commentary by Gervasio Fernandes de Queiroga, *CNBB: Comunhao e Corresponsabilidade* (Sao Paulo: Paulinas, 1977). "Corresponsibility" in this context refers to unified pastoral planning and action on the part of the hierarchy on a nationwide level, as well as to the more democratic relations between bishops and priests. An equivalent term might be "collegiality."

[6]These suggestions included parish decentralization and an increase in the ecclesial role of the laity.

[7]A social institution is an established pattern of human interaction. To institutionalize a new religious form means to make it an established feature of

official church policy and teaching. This makes the new form more solid or more permanent, and no longer a mere contingency measure. Once the preferential option for the poor became institutionalized within Brazilian Catholicism (through the Unified Pastoral Plan), it was no longer simply a means of combatting Communism by means of a social program instituted in cooperation with a democratic government. In fact, in the context of the military dictatorship after 1964, the option for the poor actually led many of the bishops to take official positions that would place them in *opposition* to the government.

[8]This development illustrates the relative autonomy of religion in relation to other social institutions (such as the government and the economy). This means that religion is neither a world unto itself nor a mere reflection of the political-economic context. Rather it responds to an external stimulus, creating an institutionalized pattern by means of which it then acts back upon the social context, even if that context is now different from the one which generated the original stimulus (see note 7 above).

[9]The Economy and Humanism movement was begun in France by the Dominican priest Louis Joseph Lebret. Father Lebret introduced the movement to Brazil in 1947. It was a lay movement in the sense that it was administratively autonomous in relation to the Church. Its membership included both priests and lay persons. The main work of Economy and Humanism in Brazil was a series of social research projects, all in the state of São Paulo. But the influence of the movement went beyond this. Many members were also Catholic Actionists, especially JOCists and JUCists. Father Lebret himself had a great deal of influence among Catholic Actionists (many of whom read his books). He was also a good friend of Dom Hélder Câmara, with whom he likely had a mutual influence. The impact of Economy and Humanism on the Church in Brazil was in the deepening of the consciousness of the importance of dealing with social-economic problems. Its influence beyond the Church ws particularly strong in the universities and in the press, through the persons who worked in it (mostly students and professionals in law, medicine and engineering). The movement was strong until 1966. It ceased to exist in Brazil because of the particularly severe repression against its members. (This information came from interviews with former members of Economy and Humanism in Brazil.)

[10]Conferencia Nacional dos Bispos do Brasil (CNBB), *Plano de Pastoral de Conjunto* (Rio de Janeiro: Livraria Dom Bosco Editora, 1966) [Unified Pastoral Plan], pp. 25, 26.

[11]Unified Pastoral Plan, pp. 28-30.

[12]For examples of this "self-preservation model," see Ivan Vallier, *Catholicism, Social Control, and Modernization in Latin America* (Englewood Cliffs, N.J.: Prentice-Hall, 1970) and Thomas C. Bruneau, *The Political Transformation of the Brazilian Catholic Church* (London: Cambridge University Press, 1974).

[13]Unified Pastoral Plan, pp. 53, 99.

[14]*Ibid.*, p. 55.

[15]*Ibid.*, pp. 103-104.

[16]*Ibid.*, p. 55.

[17]*Ibid.*, pp. 38-39.

[18]This passage, the one which follows it and others in Part IV, Section 3, are from the notes which I took at various church gatherings in Brazil, ranging from local parish meetings to large regional assemblies of representatives from basic communities.

[19]Clodovis Boff, "A Influência Política das Comunidades Eclesiais de Base (CEBs)" (*Religiao e Sociedade* 4, 1979), pp. 95-119.

[20]Lest this passage convey the erroneous impression that the function of religious women is uniform throughout Brazil, I must hasten to add that I also met nuns who taught in private girls' schools, lived in traditional convents and wore religious habits. I have a vivid recollection of some of these traditional sisters attending a liturgy side-by-side with their more activist counterparts, who wear secular dress and who live among the poor in a little house without modern amenities.

[21]The "accompanying" of a basic ecclesial community refers to the facilitating by a middle-class pastoral agent of both spiritual formation (through the use of Scripture) and the political conscientization, but without dominating the process.

[22]Socialization is the process by which people, from early childhood, are taught the values and behaviors considered appropriate to their particular society. Sex-role socialization refers to the teaching of those characteristics that are considered specific to one's gender, for example, the nurturance of women and the aggressiveness of men.

[23]This priest seemed to be giving spontaneous lectures consisting of a sophisticated Marxian analysis of imperialism, multinational corporations, the Brazilian national debt and the international Monetary Fund.

[24]See Chapter Five.

[25]See Appendix IV for statistics on native and foreign clergy.

[26]The "organic intellectual" is a concept originated by Antonio Gramisci to designate a person who helps a class of people to articulate their world view. Pastoral agents in Latin America frequently serve this function in relation to people of the poorer classes, helping them to develop a consciousness of their oppression and mobilizing them for action.

10
A TIME OF TERROR AND A PERIOD OF GROWTH

I. The Development of the Military Regime
(1964-1970)

For about eighteen months after the coup, it was not totally clear whether there would be, as with previous interventions of the Brazilian army, a return to civilian government, and possibly even constitutional democracy, or the establishment of a long-term military dictatorship. Although each successive military president would promise a return to democracy, the provisions of the Second Institutional Act of October, 1965, made that possibility seem remote. According to this act, succeeding presidents were to be "elected" by Congress (actually they would be elected within the military and later approved by a Congress made docile by the removal of its dissident members); the president was given the power to intervene directly in states' affairs[1] and to annul the mandates of federal and state deputies; all political parties were dissolved, except for the government party, ARENA, and one carefully controlled opposition party, the MDB.[2]

In addition to the loss of political rights, there were changes in economic policy that would result in increased human suffering. One of Castello Branco's first decrees was the abolition of the mobile wage scale. This had been a measure to compensate for Brazil's high-speed inflation by granting frequent redefinitions of the minimum wage. The elimination of this measure quickly reduced real wages. There was also a rapid bankrupting of many small businessmen through the withdrawal of government credits from Brazilian firms which failed to show high productivity, leading to their replacement by North American multinational corporations. The position of these multinationals was further strengthened by means of an agreement with USAID by which the Brazilian government gave a guarantee against every kind of loss to which the North American companies might be subject, including breach of contract, revolution and even inflation. Damages were to be paid in dollars. In general, the new government's economic policies clearly favored North American interests at the expense both of Brazilian entrepreneurs and of Brazilian workers.

Successive institutional acts continued to strengthen the position of the military regime, and, in 1967, the National Security Law and a new constitution both provided a legal basis for the establishment of a repressive police state. The National Security Law, which went into effect on March 17, 1967 (two days after General Costa e Silva became president) included fifty-eight articles, the violation of which would be judged by military tribunals. Among the provisions were sentences of up to two years' imprisonment for journalists who published any news considered to be a threat to national security, and up to six years' imprisonment for any worker who took part in a strike in what the military tribunal judged to be essential services.

The new constitution severely reduced the powers of Congress, allowing the president to legislate by decree and multiplying the number of permissible cases of federal intervention into internal matters of the states. The SNI (National Information Service, the central organ of the military police) was given broad powers, permitting it to function as a type of Brazilian Gestapo.

These measures did not prevent the re-emergence, in 1968, of student, worker and peasant movements, as well as the continuation of terrorist activities (such as the kidnapping of ambassadors) by the urban guerrillas. The regime's response was conspicuously repressive of the student movement — universities were invaded by the police, who made massive arrests. Eight hundred students were arrested at the UNE congress in October, 1968. Furthermore, the government decreed that any "lapse of discipline" among students would result in immediate and permanent expulsion.

The brief reappearance of the popular movements helped to fuel congressional opposition to the military government. Meanwhile, one congressman in particular, Márcio Moreira Alves, who was also a journalist, had been working for four years to document and publish numerous accounts of torture and had even managed to get into the notorious penitentiary in Recife to interview victims.[4] After Alves made a speech in which he criticized the Army, the government demanded authorization from Congress for proceedings against him. Their refusal to do so provided the government with a pretext for silencing Congress. In December 1968, Costa e Silva signed the Fifth Institutional Act, which effectively removed any remaining obstacles to the absolute rule by the president and the military police. The latter immediately began a systematic attack on the urban guerrilla groups, subjecting all those captured to severe torture. However, this punishment was not reserved for known guerrillas. Torture was used against every prisoner even vaguely suspected of contact with clandestine organizations. And yet, the worst was still to come.

In August 1969, President Costa e Silva suffered a serious stroke, and it was evident to a small group of generals that he would not be able to continue as president. To avoid succession by the civilian vice-president, they concealed the president's condition long enough to form themselves into a junta, sidestepping the constitution by means of yet another institutional act. They declared that now only generals could vote for the president and that only a four-star general could be elected. Thus Garrastazu Médici, head of the SNI, became president of Brazil. The Congress (which had been suspended for over a year) was called in to ratify the "election."

Under Médici, the repression was intensified to the point of producing a reign of pure terror. Thousands of people were arrested and tortured as a matter of routine. Prisoners could legally be held incommunicado for ten days. A new law, which punished subversion with death, could be used not only against armed insurgents but also against journalists and anyone else perceived by the military to be a threat against "national security." The victims of the repression included many lay Catholic militants, as well as priests, religious and sometimes even bishops. Between 1968 and 1973, there were at least 395 known arrests and 34 documented cases of torture among clergy, religious and lay persons engaged in Church activities. Thirteen persons, including bishops, were abducted, over 140 were indicted for various "crimes" and seven priests and over 200 lay persons were killed.[5] Not surprisingly, the bishops began to reconsider their 1964 position of support of the military regime. But even before the documents of denunciation began to be published, there was being prepared another phenomenon that would have a profound effect on the articulation of the preferential option for the poor — the meeting of the Latin American bishops at Medellín.

II. Medellín

The Latin American Bishops Conference (CELAM) was created largely at the initiative of Dom Hélder Câmara and his Chilean friend, Dom Manuel Larraín, during the Eucharistic Congress of 1955 in Rio de Janeiro. Both bishops were instrumental in preparing the Second General Conference of Latin American Bishops (CELAM II) that was held in Medellín, Colombia in 1968, although Dom Manuel died shortly before that historic event.

According to an official account,[6] the idea for the Medellín Conference originated in Rome in 1965, at the end of the Second Vatican Council. Dom Manuel, who at the time was president of CELAM, felt that the time had come to gather the bishops of Latin America for the purpose of adapting the Church there to the decisions of the Council and to the current social and religious conditions of their continent. The subsequent death of Dom Manuel left Dom Hélder in a key role among the 130 voting bishops and priests and fifteen theological consultants at Medellín (fifteen of the voting members and four of the theological consultants were Brazilian).[7]

The involvement of Dom Hélder in both the creation of CELAM and the preparation for Medellín is significant. It provides an example of another important ecclesial event (a previous one was Vatican II) in which there was a strong Brazilian input into a hierarchical position that would then influence the Church in Brazil even further, revitalizing it in its process toward the development of the preferential option for the poor. Penny Lernoux[8] has suggested that the majority of the bishops at Medellín followed the lead of such progressives as Dom Hélder and Dom Manuel without being fully aware of the revolutionary implications of the concluding documents. It is difficult to know whether Dom Hélder was conscious of his key role in an assembly of churchmen who had no intention of doing anything particularly radical. When interviewed, Dom Hélder tends to give all credit to the Holy Spirit. Another interviewee, however, seemed to indicate that the quiet, humble archbishop of Recife and a small group of advisors were in some way conspiring to move the Church ahead.

> There were a core group of people around Dom Hélder who were fermenting something as far as Church and religion go in Brazil. . . Medellín was the result of what was going on in Brazil. It is so important to understand the presence of Dom Hélder — that it was already going on, and that Medellín was a result, and that he was 'way ahead of them. When the bishops got together at Medellín, he . . . had his own people put it together. I remember that, a few years later, some felt that they had been "taken" — *some* of them — by Dom Hélder. But it was too late. The Medellín documents were out.
>
> (A missionary priest)

CELAM II was officially opened by Pope Paul VI on August 24, 1968, during the Eucharistic Congress in Bogotá. It was continued by the bishops in Medellín from August 26 to September 5. There had been extensive preparation during the three years since Dom Manuel and Dom Hélder had first discussed the idea of the conference. The results of the preparation were evident in the working draft and seven position papers.[9] The conclusions were written up in the form of sixteen documents, five of which were in the category of human promotion[10] and eleven in evangelization.

The introduction to the working document states that it was prepared by a group of *peritos* (literally "experts" — probably referring to theologians and sociologists) who had been invited by CELAM to a meeting in Bogotá the previous January. The document outlines the difficult social and religious realities of Latin America, notes the efforts of some bishops in human rights and admits that the Church as a whole has not done enough. It makes explicit the unity of spiritual and social concerns in the process of eternal salvation.

> Through his work in the world, man fulfills himself, and at the same time, transcends himself. He enters ever deeper into Christ's salvation while offering it to others, too. In collaboration with God, he goes about his activities: creating a more just and brotherly world . . . "The Christian who neglects his temporal duties neglects his duties toward his neighbor, and even God, and jeopardizes his eternal salvation."[11] [Section in quotation marks is from the Vatican II document, *Gaudium et Spes*.]

Another Brazilian bishop who appears to have had considerable influence at Medellín was Dom Eugênio Sales. It seems significant that the originator of the Natal Movement prepared the position paper on human promotion and likely had influence with the committee that prepared the final document on justice. Dom Eugênio's paper advocated basic communities, cooperatives, unions and conscientization at the grassroots.[12] These same elements appeared in the document on justice:

> Therefore, in the intermediary professional structure the peasants' and workers' unions, to which the workers have a right, should acquire sufficient strength and power. . . . We must awaken the social conscience and communal customs in all strata of society and professional groups regarding such values as dialogue and community living within the same group and relations with wider social groups (workers, peasants, professionals, clergy, religious, administrators, etc.).
>
> This task of "conscientización" and social education

ought to be integrated into joint Pastoral Action at various levels. . . .

It is necessary that small basic communities be developed in order to establish a balance with minority groups, which are the groups in power. This is only possible through vitalization of these very communities by means of the natural innate elements in their environment.

(Document on Justice, Articles 12, 17, 20)

The dual function of the basic communities — human promotion and evangelization — is evident in the fact that they are also advocated in the documents on Pastoral Care of the Masses and on Joint Pastoral Planning.

That a greater number of ecclesial communities be formed in the parishes, particularly in rural and marginal urban communities. These must have as their foundation the Word of God and, insofar as possible, find their fulfillment in the Eucharistic celebration, always in communion with and dependent upon the local bishop.

(Document on Pastoral Care of the Masses, Article 13)

The Christian ought to find the living of the communion, to which he has been called, in his "base community," that is to say, in a community, local or environmental, which corresponds to the reality of a homogeneous group and whose size allows for personal fraternal contact among its members.

(Document on Joint Pastoral Planning, Article 10)

Medellín did not stop at the level of Christian community

but also advocated certain basic social reforms, including the redistribution of land and the participation of poor people in their own betterment (which the bishops termed "human promotion," in contrast to traditional almsgiving).

> The Second Episcopal Conference wishes to voice its pastoral concern for the extensive peasant class, which, although included in the above remarks, deserves urgent attention because of its special characteristics. If it is true that one ought to consider the diversity of circumstances and resources in the different countries, there is no doubt that there is a common denominator in all of them: the need for the human promotion of the peasants and Indians. This uplifting will not be visible without an authentic and urgent reform of agrarian structures and policies. This structural change and its political implications go beyond a simple distribution of land. It is indispensable to make an adjudication of such lands, under detailed conditions which legitimize their occupation and insure their productivity for the benefit of the families and the national economy. This will entail, aside from juridical and technical aspects not within our competence, the organization of the peasants into effective intermediate structures, principally in the form of cooperatives; and motivation towards the creation of urban centers in rural areas which would afford the peasant population the benefits of culture, health, recreation, spiritual growth, participation in local decisions, and in those which have to do with the economy and national politics.
>
> (Document on Justice, Article 14)

The Medellín documents thus represent a strong statement by the Latin American hierarchy on the following subjects: the unacceptability of the state of poverty and repression in which millions of people are forced to live; the necessity of social change, particularly land reform; the advocacy of popular organizations, such as unions and cooperatives; the political participation of peasants; and the encouragement of basic ecclesial communities, for both social and pastoral reasons. The bishops did not advocate violent revolution or socialism. In fact, the document on Peace (Article 19) states that violent revolutions will only generate new injustices. However, there are other statements in that document that could be interpreted as qualifications against absolute pacifism:

(1) justice is a prerequisite for peace (Article 16);

(2) one should not be surprised that there is a temptation to violence, because most of the people have been bearing an intolerable situation (Article 16);

(3) persons in power who use violence against peaceful efforts for change will be responsible for the consequent eruptions of violence among the oppressed (Article 17).

Although the bishops indicted both capitalism and socialism for militating against human dignity, they appeared to see the solution to the problem in the reform of capitalism. They appealed to businessmen and political authorities to modify their attitudes and behavior. No similar appeal was made to socialists.

> The system of liberal capitalism and the temptation of the Marxist system would appear to exhaust the possibilities of transforming the economic structures of our continent. Both systems militate against the dignity of the human person. One takes for granted the primacy of capital, its power and its discriminatory utilization in the function of profit-making. The other, although it ideologically supports a kind of

humanism, is more concerned with collective man,
and in practice becomes a totalitarian concentration
of state power. We must denounce the fact that Latin
America sees itself caught between these two options
and remains dependent on one or the other of the
centers of power which control its economy.

Therefore, on behalf of Latin America, we make
an urgent appeal to the businessmen, to their organizations and to political authorities, so that they
might radically modify the evaluation, the attitudes
and the means regarding the goal, organization and
functioning of business. All those financiers deserve
encouragement who, individually or through their
organizations, make an effort to conduct their business according to the guidelines supplied by the social teachings of the Church.

(Document on Justice, Article 10)

By the standards of contemporary liberation theologians,
Medellín was quite mild. At most it represented liberal reformism.[14] However, in contrast to the traditional position of the
Latin American Catholic Church on the side of the landed and
military elites, Medellín was revolutionary. First of all, it advocated land reform. Second, it took a strong position on the side
of the poor, not in the sense of advocating almsgiving but rather
in the encouragement of measures leading to their greater social
and political participation (human promotion). Third, it provided a potential for change within the Church itself, by means
of the basic communities. These communities, because they
incorporated elements of lay leadership and parish decentralization, would produce a tendency toward the re-thinking of
authority relations within the Church. Although there have
been no official statements (from Medellín or elsewhere) that
would encourage such questioning, the experiences of the basic
ecclesial communities do produce a certain confidence in lay

authority, thus containing an implicit challenge to the bishops' monopoly of religious power. The extent to which the lay poor will take up this challenge remains to be seen.

Medellín was significant as the institutionalization of the preferential option for the poor throughout Latin America. It gave continental legitimation for tendencies begun in individual countries. Although Brazil was not the only country where social projects and basic communities existed (similar things were being done in Chile and Panama), the Church in Brazil was the most advanced along these lines, had pioneered the national bishops' conference and unified pastoral planning and, through such persons as Dom Eugênio, Dom Hélder and the latter's theological advisors, had had a conspicuous influence on the Medellín conference. In this light, the institutionalization of the preferential option for the poor could be said to have occurred as follows:

(1) pastoral experiments in Brazil, such as the Natal Movement;

(2) institutionalization by the CNBB in the Unified Pastoral Plan of 1965;

(3) institutionalization by CELAM in the Medellín documents.

So far this analysis has focused on the social and religious factors that led up to the development of the preferential option for the poor. An important element in this process was the Church's capacity to adapt and survive in the face of changes in the social context. However, with the institutionalization of the option for the poor, a new dynamic was set in motion. This option would become an integral part of Latin American Catholic belief, particularly since it was compatible with the teachings of Vatican II and with the encyclicals of Pope John XXIII and Pope Paul VI.[15] This is important because:

(1) The preferential option for the poor would be a relatively autonomous element, whose continuation would no longer be dependent on the perception of a Communist threat. This would be particularly significant in countries such as Brazil, where military repression had eliminated such a threat.

(2) This new feature, now institutionalized and thus possessing its own dynamic, could become a source of religious influence on external social processes (for example, social activism and social change).

(3) The institutionalization of the preferential option for the poor at Medellín would be a widespread source of legitimation for the most progressive theologians and pastoral agents in Latin America, some of whom would push the option far beyond the liberal reformist intentions of the bishops. This revolutionizing tendency would become most evident in the activities of the basic ecclesial communities in Central America and in the integration of Catholic belief with Marxian sociology within the theology of liberation.[16]

In Brazil, some of these tendencies were thwarted by the repression that became most severe shortly after Medellín. Because of press censorship, theologians were not even able to publish works in which the word "liberation" appeared. So liberation theology, which had some of its origins in Brazil, would flourish in other countries instead.[17] On the practical grassroots level, the revolutionary potential in the Brazilian rural and urban labor movements was mitigated by the government control of all unions. But somehow, the little basic communities slipped past the government's control.

III. Basic Ecclesial Communities: A Space for Dissent

With the institutionalization of the basic ecclesial communities, there would be some important changes in the continuing process of their development. For one thing, their numbers would increase much more rapidly. By 1980, the estimates for the number of CEBs in Brazil alone were running as high as eighty thousand.[18] For another thing, there would be changes in the locations and functions of the CEBs. Previously they had existed mainly in rural areas, where initially they were accepted by the bishops as a means of compensating for the shortage of clergy and of defending the faith against Communism. By the late 1960's, however, the CEBs were being encouraged as a means of reaching out to the people living in misery on the periphery of São Paulo (now the location of the greatest concentration of basic communities in all of Brazil).

> 1968 was the point of acceptance of the basic communities as a method of revitalizing the Church by means of a growing participation by the people.
> . . . At that time I was already in São Paulo as an auxiliary bishop. So I started the formation of these nuclei. When I became archbishop, I proposed that we start what was called "Operation Periphery," so that there could be created in all parts of the periphery community centers where the people who arrive (i.e., migrants from other parts of Brazil) could meet and organize. This almost always resulted in a basic ecclesial community. . . . After I was able to sell the palace, we had four million dollars for the centers.
>
> (Dom Paulo Evaristo Arns,
> Cardinal-Archbishop of São Paulo)

The rapid growth of the CEBs in São Paulo is a function of another dimension of the CEBs that resulted from Medellín — that is, that now they would more frequently represent an innovation coming "from the top down." In other words, rather than being mainly a grassroots creation, facilitated by pastoral agents acting on their own initiative and approved after-the-fact, or not approved, by their bishop, the CEBs would now more often be created by the pastoral agents acting on a direc-tive from the bishop. This point is well illustrated by the follow-ing excerpt from an interview with Florence Anderson, a Scrip-ture scholar who, along with a Dominican priest, Frei G. S. Gorgulho, assisted Cardinal Arns in his work on the urban periphery:

> In 1967, Dom Paulo invited us to work on an evangeli-zation program. And we worked from '67 to '70, reach-ing more than five thousand communities. When he was nominated archbishop, he asked us to do for the archdiocese what we had done in the north region . And now the two of us are responsible for the coor-dination of the basic Christian communities in São Paulo.

It should be clear that in the archdiocese of São Paulo the impetus for the development of the CEBs came from the ar-chbishop, for example, in his recruiting of two Biblical scholars to help with the evangelization program and in the selling of his own residence to provide funds for community centers in which groups of poor people could meet. The subsequent in-teraction between hierarchy and grassroots was well explained by an active Catholic lay person who has lived for many years on the periphery of the city:

> The idea of the basic ecclesial communities was not a discovery of the Christian people themselves. It was a proposal from the top down — but it was a proposal that caught on well.
>   (A factory worker and organizer of CEBs)

From the viewpoint of the bishops who encouraged the forma-tion of basic communities, their main purpose was evangelization. However, in the context of the extreme political repression after 1968, the CEBs also began to play a new political role. Paradoxically, this was possible because they did not appear to be "political." After the conspicuous militancy of JUC, the CEBs appeared tame, both to the conservatives among the hierarchy and to the military regime. They simply looked like groups of pious people who, with the approval of their priests and bishops, were meeting together to study the Bible. What actually went on in many of these groups, however, would be something a bit different.

One of the key concepts encouraged at Medellín was conscientization. It was at Medellín that this method, which had previously been used by Church people to develop social and political consciousness, was integrated with Biblical study. So, although it may have appeared to government authorities that the CEBs were rather traditional evangelical groups, they were actually engaged in the business of conscientization. They became a space within the Church where people could develop their consiousness, their sense of participation, their self-expression and ability to dialogue and, finally, the expression of their protest against the injustice of their situation. They became a space where the critical spirit could survive. This situation would already be well-developed by the time that the military regime became fully aware of it.

Conscientization, as practiced in the basic communities, affected not only the lay members but also pastoral agents and bishops. Obviously the most immediate contact was between the people and the pastoral agents. The particular dynamic by which the method of conscientization is carried out requires that the middle-class lay person, sister or priest *listen* to poor people. In this way, they have learned the details of the experience of oppression, and they have also learned about simple faith. Both pastoral agents and bishops have spoken of how much they have learned from the people.

As I was helping the people to re-read their reality, they were teaching me to re-read my own . . . And some Scripture scholars who live and work in Brazil have taken that perspective of the poor people in interpreting the Bible and liberation.

(A missionary sister)

We learn from the people. For example, if I have contact with the people, I experience their goodness. The evangelizer is evangelized. We are saved together.

(Dom José Lamartine Soares, Auxiliary Bishop of Olinda/Recife

Some members of the hierarchy have made the effort to establish contact with the people at the grassroots.[19] Others have learned the people's viewpoint through pastoral agents who are themselves listening to the poor. Still other bishops have become aware of injustice through experiences of repression, either because of their own harassment by the military or because of the torture or murder of a priest or other Church worker. In any case, the way was being opened for the hierarchy itself to become a dissident element within Brazilian society.

IV. The Bishops: Conscientization and Consequences

A recurring theme both in the literature and in my interviews is the "conversion of bishops." Over and over again, it is pointed out that most of the bishops were originally in favor of the coup, but that many of them changed their view within a few years. This change in viewpoint is usually connected with two factors — contact with the military and contact with the poor.

Archbishop Lorscheider, who became Secretary General of the CNBB, was middle-of-the-road, although respected by all. One day he was giving a talk at the Catholic University in Rio. The federal troops, not knowing he was there at all, swooped in and took them all off. He was in jail and saw for himself what was happening.

(A missionary priest)

I could tell you about a lot of radical bishops who had been in favor of the coup of 1964. . . . There was one of them that was sent up to the north of Brazil, to a diocese with a really hot situation — big landowners, a lot of poor people — because he was conservative . . . easy to get along with. He says that one day he was riding down a country road, and these very poor rural workers got out in the middle of the road, stopped his horse, and said to him, "Are you with the landowners, or are you with us?" Now his whole idea of being a priest was that he wasn't "with" anybody. He believed in listening to both sides and trying to get people together so that the situation would not explode. But when he looked down at those desperate faces, he thought to himself, "How can I tell these people that I am not with them?" And from that moment, his whole idea of what it meant to be a priest, to be a bishop, changed.

(A lay pastoral agent)

First-hand accounts of similar experiences have been given by several Brazilian bishops.[20] The pattern that usually emerges is as follows: the cruelty of the military regime, combined with the increasing impoverishment and the emerging consciousness of the poor people, moved these bishops from a position in support of the coup to one of prophetic denunciation.

As they began to learn from the people in the basic communities,
they caught up with their colleagues who had earlier learned
from the lay militants in specialized Catholic Action (such as
Dom Hélder Câmara, one of the few Brazilian bishops who
never appeared to be in support of the coup). Thus the pastoral
innovations of the 1950's, Vatican II, the pastoral plans, Medellín and the military repression of the late 1960's all culminated
in the emergence of a new way of being Church. In Brazil there
is a visible minority of bishops, growing in numbers and influence, who have made a commitment to the preferential option
for the poor. This commitment is expressed in the strong denunciations of government policy expressed in pastoral documents
and in their encouragement of the basic ecclesial communities.

NOTES

[1]An example of federal intervention into affairs of the states was the appointment of many state governors by the military regime.

[2]Although the MDB (Brazilian Democratic Movement) had been a fairly
progressive party, in the context of the authoritarian military regime, it was
an "opposition party" in name only. Rather than a true two-party system,
Philippe Schmitter (in "The 'Portugalization' of Brazil," Alfred Stepan, Ed.,
Authoritarian Brazil: Origins, Policies, and Future. New Haven: Yale University Press, p. 210) termed the Brazilian system after 1964 a one-and-a-half
party system, in which "the predominance of the official party, the *Aliança
Renovadora Nacional* (ARENA) over the opposition *Movimento Democrático
Brasileiro* (MDB) had to be guaranteed by periodic purge and manipulation
by the executive."

[3]José Quartim, *Dictatorship and Armed Struggle in Brazil* (London: NLB,
1971) pp. 57-59. Much of the information in this section is from this book,
particularly pages 56 through 75.

[4]See Márcio Moreira Alves, *A Grain of Mustard Seed* (Harmondsworth, England: Penquin Books, 1973), pp. 83-84.

[5]Latin American Documentation (LADOC), *Repression Against the Church
in Brazil: 1968-1978,* LADOC Keyhole Series, No. 18 (Washington, D.C.: United
States Catholic Conference, 1978), pp. 16-21.

[6]Frei Bonaventura Kloppenburg, O.F.M., editor of the *Brazilian Ecclesiastical Review* at the time of the Medellín conference, writing in the December, 1968, issue of that journal.

[7]Luis Alberto Gómez de Souza, *Classes Populares e Igreja nos Caminhos da História* (Petrópolis: Vozes, 1982), p. 291.

[8]Penny Lernoux, *The Cry of the People* (Garden City, N.Y.: Doubleday, 1980), p. 42.

[9]The working draft for Medellín may be found in English in *Between Honesty and Hope* (Peruvian Bishops' Commission for Social Action. Maryknoll, N.Y.: Maryknoll Publications, 1969), pp. 171-192. The seven position papers may be found in Latin American Bishops' Conference (CELAM), *The Church in the Present-Day Transformation of Latin America in the Light of the Council* [Medellín Documents] (Bogotá: General Secretariat of CELAM, 1970), pp. 79-280.

[10]"Human promotion" is a term used in the Latin American Catholic Church to refer to the social betterment of the poorer classes by means of their greater participation in political, economic, and cultural life. This concept implies both a concern for the total person (rather than exclusively religious or exclusively economic) and a respect for the initiative of the people themselves. This concept of human promotion stands in sharp contrast to the traditional notion of assistentialism, which made poor people the passive recipients of alms from the wealthy and did not question the injustice of the political-economic structures that make some people rich and others poor.

[11]Working draft of Medellín (see note 9), Article 11.4.

[12]See Dom Eugênio Sales, in CELAM, (*op. cit.* — see note 9), Position Papers for Medellín, pp. 545-547.

[13]CELAM, *op. cit.*, p. 80.

[14]I have referred to the position of the bishops at Medellín as "liberal reformism" because they did not oppose the capitalist system as a whole (or advocate a change to socialism) but rather seemed to be appealing to the consciences of businessmen and other people of power (for example, political authorities) to correct the abuses within the existing system. Contemporary liberation theologians do not appear to have any such faith in the capitalist system, or in the good intentions of those who profit from it. Instead, they have incorporated into their theology certain elements of Marxian sociology, specifically:
(1) a strong class analysis, with particular reference to the two fundamental classes — bourgeoisie and proletariat, the latter including both factory workers and rural workers;
(2) the belief in the poor as the source of true consciousness (which, in the theology, translates to listening to the poor in their application of Scripture to their social realities); the assertion that liberation theology must come from the poor themselves, as only they are capable of working out revolutionary

utopias, rather than bourgeois-reformist ideologies.

(3) an image of utopian society (based on humanistic socialism) and a sense of the dialectical tension between that which presently exists and that which is to come;

(4) a belief in the positive function of conflict as a means for resolving divergent dualisms;

(5) the inclusion of political liberation within the concept of salvation;

(6) the advocacy of an attitude of both criticism and self-criticism.

(See Gutierrez, *op. cit.*; L. Boff, *op. cit.*; Cussianovich, *op. cit.*)

[15]The Vatican II document most often cited is *Gaudium et Spes* (Pastoral Constitution on the Church in the Modern World). Among papal encyclicals, the ones considered to be the most applicable to "human promotion" in Latin America are *Pacem in Terris* (Peace on Earth) and *Mater et Magistra* (Mother and Teacher) by Pope John XXIII, and *Populorum Progressio* (On the Development of Peoples), by Pope Paul VI.

[16]See note 14 above for a discussion of the incorporation of Marxian sociology into liberation theology.

[17]Some of the best-known theologians are from Peru (Gutierrez and Cussianovich), Chile (Galilea, Munoz and Comblin — who was born in Belgium and went to Chile after being denied re-entry into Brazil, to which he finally returned in 1982), Argentina (Dussel, Scannone and Miguez Bonino) and Mexico (Vidales and Miranda). It is the Brazilian theologian Leonardo Boff who, in the preface to the English translation of his book *Jesus Christ Liberator,* wrote of the restrictions on what could be published in Brazil.

[18]Lernoux, *op. cit.,* p. 41; Thomas Sanders, "The Catholic Church in Brazil's Political Transition" (Hanover, N.H.: American Universities Field Staff Reports), p. 8.

[19]Among the bishops directly in touch with people at the grassroots are Dom António Fragaso, who solicits input from CEB members for pastoral planning in his diocese of Crateús; Dom Hélder Câmara, who has office hours one afternoon each week, when anyone may come in to speak with him without an appointment; Dom Angélico Sândalo Bernardino, the auxiliary bishop responsible for the eastern zone on the periphery of São Paulo, whom I observed at a regional meeting to which hundreds of representatives of CEBs had come to give him their input into pastoral planning. A priest in São Paulo told me that there are at least thirty Brazilian bishops who have made a commitment to consulting the CEBs in pastoral planning.

[20]See Helena Salem, *A Igreja dos Oprimidos* (São Paulo: Brasil Debates, 1981), pp. 119-150.

11
DIMENSIONS OF THE PREFERENTIAL OPTION FOR THE POOR

I. Pastoral Documents

There are numerous ways, both formal and informal, in which the bishops spoke out against the regime. The most significant, because they represent an institutionalization of prophetic denunciations, are the written documents that were signed by regional groups of bishops or by a representative commission of the CNBB or that were presented at an assembly of bishops (such as Dom Cándido Padin's statement on the Doctrine of National Security[1]). These documents are notable in the integration of their protest with Church teaching. They all cite at least some of the following: Scripture, Documents of Vatican II (particularly *Gaudium et Spes*), papal encyclicals and other statements by popes (especially Pope John XXIII and Pope John Paul VI, although the latest documents also cite Pope John Paul II) and CELAM documents — from Medellín and, more recently, from Puebla.[2]

Two main themes run through the documents: protest against repression and protest against the increasing impoverishment of the people. The protests against repression run the whole range from accounts of harassment of bishops, priests, religious and lay people to the witness against murders by military authorities or by civilians who act with impunity, as well as more general statements about human rights.

> Dona Margarida Barbosa was imprisoned from the fifth to the eleventh of this month and tortured by the police, who made her kneel on bottle caps, with arms stretched out. They inserted needles under her finger nails and in her breasts and beat her. The interrogation was done at gun point, and she was given no food or water while it lasted. On October 22, at 5 p.m., her cries of "Don't hit me!" were heard from the street.
>
> Her niece, Dona Santana, was arrrested at the same time and was raped by several soldiers, who also burned her husband's house, fields and a silo full of rice.
>
> The suffering of these women was the reason why Dom Pedro [Casadáliga, bishop of São Felix] and Pe. João Bosco went to the police station at Ribeirão Bonito. There they tried to have a calm dialogue with Corporals Juraci and Messias and with two soldiers, interceding for the victims. The police reacted with insults and threats if they should dare to denounce these abuses. They hit the priest in the face with a rifle butt and shot him in the head with a dumdum bullet.
>
> During the three hours he remained conscious, Pe. João Bosco received the sacraments and offered his sufferings to God for the people, and especially for the Indians. Taken to the city of Goiânia, he died at 5 p.m. on October 12.[3]

The document just quoted, which was written in 1976, contained the first harsh criticism of the regime by the CNBB as a whole. Coming after eight years of the period of the most intense repression in recent Brazilian history (1968-1978), it perhaps illustrates the length of time needed for a large organization to act in a prophetic manner. However, statements by individual bishops came much sooner, as is illustrated by the following passage from the presentation made by Dom Cándido Padin at the July, 1968, meeting of the CNBB:

> In Brazil today is emerging a new version of the "master race." This master race will make decisions about the instruments of economic power and over-developed technology, with domination by both, one guaranteeing the other. [The master race] will try to take over and exploit the weak and underde-veloped masses. And a general method for taking over the weaker nations seems to be to transform them into military states that are easily manipu-lated. The methods are the same as those of Nazism, but more refined through experience. An unmen-tioned goal will perhaps be the annihilation of the Church [earlier Dom Padin had quoted Hitler's *Mein Kampf* regarding the Church], which, once again, may be the only element able to oppose this state of affairs.[4]

This passage may have been prophetic in both senses of the word — denunciatory and predictive. For the authoritarian state did persecute the Brazilian Catholic Church in the following years, and the Church did become the only institution able to express protest, both in regard to the persecution of its own members and hierarchy and in regard to human rights in general.

The first official statements criticizing the regime for its
economic policies resulting in the increasing impoverishment
of the majority of the people came from groups of bishops in
two of the poorest regions — the northeast and the center-west.
Both utilized social scientific data to document the horrifying
socio-economic conditions in their regions. Like the Medellín
documents, these statements unify religious and social commit-
ments.

> Salvation is not, however, a reality outside of his-
> tory, in the life beyond. It starts here. Eternal life,
> although not completed, has already been given to
> us by the Son of God in human life here and now,
> together with the personal and interior dimension.
> Total human liberation is not possible unless it in-
> cludes a political reach, unless it presupposes a social
> and economic context. Therefore liberation, accord-
> ing to the plan of the Father, proceeds through and
> within the people, where it verifies the politico-social
> dimension of man. God saves each one within a
> people, "the People of God," the destination of His
> love.[5]

It would appear, from the passages about to be quoted, that
both documents moved beyond Medellín insofar as they did not
propose the reform of capitalism as a viable solution. They
placed the blame for the situation on international capitalism,
and, although they did not advocate socialism by name, their
proposed solutions sound very much like it.

> International capitalism and those who commit
> themselves to it in this country — the dominant class
> — impose, by all the means of communication and
> education, a type of dominant culture. This serves
> to justify their domination and to camouflage the

system of oppression. At the same time, they try to numb the great masses of the people, to invent a type of man that is resigned in the face of his alienation. . . . The oppressed masses of the workers, peasants and many underemployed people are still becoming aware and are progressively assuming a new liberating consciousness.

The dominated class does not have any means of liberating itself other than by means of the long and difficult journey, already begun, toward social ownership of the means of production.[6]

It is necessary to vanquish capitalism. It is the greatest evil, the accumulated sin, the deteriorating root, the tree that produces those fruits with which we are acquainted: poverty, hunger, illness, the death of the great majority. . . .

It is necessary to vanquish the fear of change. . . .

It is necessary to build a different world. We do not know exactly how it should be, but we have no confidence [in the present one]. We want a world where the fruits of labor belong to everyone. We want a world in which people work, not to make someone rich but to assure that everyone has what they need to live: food, health, housing, education, clothing, shoes, water, electricity. We want a world in which money serves people and people do not serve money. We want a world where everyone could work for everyone, rather than a divided world in which each one is out for himself. Therefore, we want a world in which there is only one people, without the division between rich and poor. We want a world where all people do everything they are able to do for the good of everyone.[7]

Bishops have not taken these positions in a vacuum. According to Dom Moacyr Grechi of the Prelacy of Acre and Purus (quoted in Salem, 1981: 157), it is frequently activism at the grassrooots that induces a bishop to take a more radical position. So it seems that some bishops have allowed poor people and pastoral agents to educate them on political-economic issues. Several bishops have also encouraged lay input into pastoral planning.

II. The Laity and Pastoral Planning

The Unified Pastoral Plan (PPC) of 1965 explicitly advocated the inclusion of lay people in parish, diocesan and regional pastoral planning processes. But there is no guarantee that each bishop will implement this particular dimension. In talking with lay people at a large gathering of CEBs from several different dioceses, I found three patterns in relation to lay input — bishops who do not encourage it at all, bishops who actively encourage it and put into practice measures that lay people suggest and bishops with a third pattern described by this speaker:

> We have a great deal of input at the parish level but practically none at all at the diocesan level. The bishop is very supportive of CEBs and their social role. However, when we go to diocesan planning meetings, we get the sense that our suggestions do not get implemented.
>
> (A member of a rural CEB in Maranhão)

An interview in another part of the country revealed a very different experience:

> Dom Angélico supports lay people completely. He attends our assemblies, gives encouragement,

speaks to our reality. Dom Angélico not only gives
strength to the lay people. He actually uses our input.
(A member of CEB on the periphery of São Paulo)

The bishop to whom this speaker referred is Dom Angélico
Sândalo Bernardino, an auxiliary bishop of São Paulo who is
responsible for the episcopal region in the eastern part of the
archdiocese. This region encompasses many poor areas on the
periphery of the city. I visited a pastoral planning assembly in
this sub-diocese of Dom Angélico's. It was held in a large hall
which was packed to capacity (at least three or four hundred
people.) There were representatives of each of the six sectors
of the region (or sub-diocese). Across the long wall were signs
labeling ten categories of pastoral work: liturgy, catechetics,
vocations, lay ministries, youth, basic communities, health, the
factory milieu, human rights and family. There were duplicate
signs for each category, indicating priorities for both the parish
level and the regional level. After a representative from each
sector gave a report on what people believed should be the
priorities, a small sign with key words was taped to the wall
below the pastoral category. So each of the six sectors gave a
total of twenty reports and put up twenty signs. It was a long
meeting but very lively, punctuated by frequent songs and some
elements of humor. With each report, there was active participation by means of discussion from the floor.

When all the reports were completed, Dom Angélico addres-
sed the assembly, thanking all for attending, commenting on
some of the proposals and stressing the importance of lay input.
At one point he paused, and apologizing for having spoken so
long (it was actually only a few minutes), asked the people's
permission to say a few more things. That permission was en-
thusiastically granted. What seemed evident in Dom Angélico's
relations with the lay people were mutual esteem and affection.

At present only about thirty of the three hundred Brazilian

bishops have made a definite commitment to seeking lay input into the process of pastoral planning.[8] However, many institutional changes in the Brazilian Catholic Church have begun with a small but vocal minority of progressive bishops. If the implementation of the lay role in this area is a growing trend, it could signal a future change in the Church, giving the lay people increasing decision-making power in relation to those areas of planning that are relevant to their area of experience — that is, the social world. As long as the experience of the majority of Brazilians is one of poverty, this lay input will help to reinforce the preferential option for the poor.

III. The Changing Role of the Basic Communities in the Catholic Church and in the Brazilian Social Reality

1. ECCLESIAL DIMENSION

The CEBs may turn out to be a perfect fit in the post-Conciliar Church in Brazil. They respond to the requirements of Vatican II for an active lay role and a concern for human social problems. Their pedagogy of conscientization permits involvement in those problems without the kind of direct political intervention that led to unholy alliances in the past. The CEBs simultaneously provide a means of dealing with the shortage of clergy and a vehicle for the evangelization of the majority of the people. They have helped to concretize the preferential option for the poor, decreasing the likelihood that some conservatives among the hierarchy would be able to reverse this position at some future time without losing the loyalty of a very large number of lay people and pastoral agents. The experience of the CEBs has also led to a subtle shift in the perception of religious authority on the part of many lay people and of some bishops. Although there has been no change in the ultimate teaching authority of the bishops (the magisterium), there are new views as to the role of the lay people.

I used to go to Church only to pray. Now I go to pray, to learn and to teach. . . . I learn from other lay people, for example, in the liturgical celebrations-without-priest, when I hear the opinions of people on the Scripture readings. . . . We used to have to obey the priest all the time. Now we are free to disagree with him. Since we are responsible members of the Church, we can tell the priest if we feel that something is not right.

(A CEB leader in São Paulo)

The priests used to be more distant, not as easy to talk with as they are now. I remember feeling so surprised the first time the bishop spoke with me. . . I feel very fulfilled and proud of my role in the Mass, with a sense of moving into a new world and of being a part of the Church along with the priests. I am also getting a sense that women are able to be active in the Church.

(Another CEB leader in São Paulo)

Has the Brazilian Church finally succeeded in reaching a compromise between lay participation and hierarchical power? There remain some questions for which there appear to be no easy answers at the present time. For example, is it likely that the CEBs in Brazil may eventually reach a crises somewhat parallel to that of JUC, although in a differnt way? The experience of the grassroots Church in Nicaragua[9] seems to indicate that the Vatican will not accept the idea that the People of God could disobey the local bishop. Will there come a point when active lay people will push the concept of the Popular Church to the extent of questioning the magesterium of the hierarchy? Or will they remain content with the lay role as presently defined, perhaps continuing to consent to be governed because of their genuine affection for some of the more progressive bishops? The history of popular religion in Brazil shows that many religious customs began through lay initiative and were only later approved by the bishops.[10] Furthermore, the continued widespread devotion to the miracle cult of Padre Cicero in Joazeiro[11] and to the many Brazilian varieties of religious syncretism indicates that popular patterns will flourish even without institutional legitimation. At the present time, however, the CEBs in Brazil are not showing signs of posing a challenge to religious authority. They seem to be thriving in many areas with progressive bishops and managing to "work around" some of the more traditional ones. Their relation to secular authority is another matter.

2. POLITICAL DIMENSION

The present and future political role of the CEBs is a matter of uncertainty and controversy among Church people and social scientists both within and outside of Brazil. First of all, it is important to make a distinction between political action and party politics. The nationwide elections of 1982 (for all offices except the presidency) led to a great surprise and a certain amount of dismay among some pastoral agents, academics and middle-class observers who had assumed that the basic communities, as a source of critical social consciousness, would automatically lead people to vote for the Workers' Party (PT), which the dismayed persons had defined as the only radical one. The election results gave most of the victories to the PDS (the government party). With the wisdom of hindsight, it is easy to offer several explanations for those results:

(1) The left was divided. PT, as a party with a strong base among urban laborers and leftist intellectuals, had a fair showing in some parts of the industrialized south (although very few actual victories) but had virtually no base at all in the rural northeast and center-west. In some of the states in those regions, a substantial number of seats for state and federal de-

puties were captured by the PMDB, the party of Miguel Arraes (governor of Pernambuco before the coup, presently a national congressman), who has always been known as a strong champion of peasant rights. Also, during my field work in the rural northeast, I noticed several households of CEB leaders that had campaign posters for the PDT, a new party which has a strongly socialist platform advocating everything from infant health to land reform to women's rights and which is the present party of Francisco Julião.

(2) A second possible explanation is that CEB members are more politically sophisticated than their middle-class observers and opted for the traditional pattern of giving the authorities what they want,[12] sensing that the defeat of the PDS would precipitate another coup and a return to severe repression. Even though the present "political opening" is less than fully democratic, there is still less terror than what existed just a few years ago. Rural poor people know that there are less conspicuous ways to exercise their political consciousness.

(3) The majority of Brazilians are cynical about party politics and/or leftist leaders; therefore electoral politics may not be an accurate indication of the real level of their political consciousness.[13]

(4) What CEBs are about is not party politics. They are about the empowerment of people as the result of the perception of their dignity derived from their reflection on Scripture. So to connect basic communities to a particular political party is to miss the whole point of their existence.

I tend to favor the last explanation, although the other three are not mere straw men. They are all plausible within the context of the Brazilian reality. However, the fourth one relates most closely to my observations and interviews. What I observed about Brazilian basic ecclesial communities that did appear intensely political was their capacity for the empowerment of people who would otherwise be marginal to the entire political-economic system. These people translate their experience of ecclesial participation to political participation. In the rural northeast, many members of CEBs are involved in land struggles with everyone from local landlords and speculators (*grileiros*) to multinational corporations attempting to dispossess people of land that their families have worked for centuries. In the center-south, CEB people on the urban periphery are involved in the labor movement, land occupations for housing, and organizing around issues of health and child care. The following excerpts from interviews with CEB members in different parts of the country provide illustrations of the range of social issues with which they are involved.

> When land problems began in this area, we already knew about them because we had received bulletins from [basic] communities in other places where there were land struggles. An "owner" came here with forged papers, claiming that this land was his. . . . Later he threatened to call in the police. We discussed the situation, and confronted him, refusing to leave. We got a lawyer. He has never been back.
>
> (A farmer in the northeast)

> The (lay) ministry school we attended taught us about both the Bible and conscientization. People from this community have been active in many local struggles — for example, the struggle to get a health center in every neighborhood. Sixty buses from the periphery took people into the city for a demonstration at the office of the Secretary of Health. There is also a day care center here because the people fought for it. We also fought for the removal of the garbage dump that used to be over there. . . . The

ministry school oriented us toward fighting for our rights.

(A housewife in the center-south)

This type of political participation is more difficult to measure than are voting patterns. First of all, some of it is clandestine, and, out of fear for their personal safety (particularly in the northeast), people may be reluctant to admit their activism to someone like a middle-class pollster or other outsider.[14] Second, their participation may be sporadic and unrecorded. In addition to the active leaders who are involved in several social projects, there are large numbers of people who may leaflet for the union one week and get on a bus for a day care center demonstration the next, without being officially registered as a member of any visible organization. The only evidence from my study of the seeming prevalence of political activity among CEB members is as follows: I made contact with prospective interviewees in different parts of Brazil by asking various pastoral agents to introduce me to persons who were active in basic ecclesial communities. In no instance did I specifically ask to meet political activists. And yet, almost invariably, the people interviewed were involved in one or more of the types of activities described above. This rather casual observation seems similar to the results of a more focused survey[15] of participants at the nationwide gathering of CEB representatives in Itaicí, São Paulo, in 1981. Out of the 163 people who responded to that questionaire, more than half were currently involved in at least one of the following struggles: neighborhood improvement, political organizing, unions, land struggles, housing, factory problems and rural cooperatives. In addition, the majority also considered themselves to be involved in Church renewal. This seems to suggest that the extent of people's involvement in grassroots movements, rather than election figures, should indicate the political consequences of the CEBs.

The present "democratic opening" raises the question of the future political role of the CEBs. Obviously, if the repression were to be resumed, the communities might return to their function as a space for conscientization and dissent. Even with the military now wise to that function, it would be difficult to suppress a multitude of small groups that could meet in different homes at different times. If the opening continues, there will likely continue a trend that is already present — for CEB members to have multiple political involvements. In such a case, while the political role of the communities may become less obvious (that is, as other options for political involvement become available with the easing up of the repression), they could still provide people with a sense of community, mutual aid and the spiritual sustenance that is helpful in maintaining a long-term struggle. In any case, it is difficult to predict the future of the CEBs and worth noting that their present political role is significant in itself. For it is through the basic communities that religious belief is contributing to movements oriented toward radical social change.

NOTES

[1]Dom Cândido Padin, "A Doutrina da Segurança Nacional à Luz da Doutrina Social da Igreja," reprinted in Luiz Gonzaga de Souza Lima, Evoluçao Política dos Católicos e da Igreja no Brasil (Petrópolis: Vozes, 1979), pp. 150-167.

[2]"Puebla" refers to the Third General Conference of the Latin American Bishops (CELAM III) held in Puebla, Mexico, in 1979.

[3]Conferência Nacional dos Bispos do Brasil (CNBB), Comunicãcao Pastoral ao Povo de Deus (São Paulo: Edições Paulinas, 1977), p. 9.

[4]Dom Candido Padin, Op. Cit., pp. 150-167.

[5]Brazilian Bishops and Religious Superiors of the Northest, Eu Ouvi os Clamores do Meu Povo (Salvador: Editora Beneditina, 1973), p. 26.

[6]Ibid., p. 29.

[7]Brazilian Bishops of the Center-West Region, "A Marginalização de um Povo," reprinted in Luiz Gonzaga de Souza Lima, *op. cit.,* pp. 237-238.

[8]See Chapter Ten, Note 9, for the source of this information.

[9]On more than one occasion, Brazilian bishops made a point to tell me that the Church in Brazil is united, and that the situation there is not as it is in Nicaragua. The manner in which their comments were made seemed to indicate sadness about the disunity between the hierarchy and the grassroots in Central America. Although there is some controversy within the Brazilian Catholic Church as to whether the "popular Church" should be encouraged, there is an important difference between that situation and the one in Nicaragua. In order to understand this difference, one must consider the particular position of the bishops within the Church. In each diocese, the bishop has authority over all the lay people, sisters, and priests, both in terms of the interpretation of doctrine and in the imposition of disciplinary measures, of which the ultimate one is excommunication. The bishop is also the link between his flock and the Pope. Nicaragua is a very small country with very few bishops. Consequently, the archbishop of Managua is a key authority figure. Brazil, on the other hand, is a large country with over three hundred bishops and several archbishops. If the archbishop of Rio de Janeiro tends to be conservative, he is balanced by the progressive archbishop of São Paulo. Furthermore, the composition of the executive committee of the National Conference of the Brazilian Bishops is important. Except for the mid-1960's, the key persons in the CNBB have tended to be progressive. The archbishop of Managua, on the other hand, tends to be relatively conservative and opposed to the present government of Nicaragua. Many people in the basic communities and their pastoral agents helped bring about the Nicaraguan revolution and are supportive of the Sandinistas — including some priests, such as Miguel D'Escoto and Ernestal Cardenal, who hold government positions. It is the archbishop of Managua, however, and not the lay people or Father D'Escoto or Father Cardenal, who has the most influence with the Vatican. It was clear from the visit of Pope John Paul II to Nicaragua in 1983 that he is not about to be favorable toward any lay people, priests or government officials who are not approved by the archbishop. The Pope's visit to Brazil was very different. There was no reprimanding of prominent clergy, nor were there any signs of disapproval of the "people's Church." In Brazil, the lay people are in unity with the bishops to the extent that the bishops are in unity with the people. One may wonder whether this unity will continue as long as the lay people do not try to push the bishops farther than they are willing to go, either in doctrine or in relations of authority.

[10]Riolando Azzi, *O Catolicismo Popular no Brasil: Aspectos Historicos* (Petrópolis: Vozes, 1978).

[11]See Ralph Della Cava, *Miracle at Joazeiro* (New York: Columbia University Press, 1970).

[12]It may be characteristic of Brazilian people of the poorer classes to tell

people in authority what they seem to want to hear, whether these authority figures be politicians, landowners, priests, social scientists or middle-class community organizers. Another example of this type of courtesy of the oppressed appears in Chapter Nine, where there is a description of a situation in which a group of rural poor people gave more traditional answers to questions about oppression after a priest had given them a sermon on the spiritual meaning of their suffering.

[13]There seems to be a North American bias in the assumption by some observers that political elections measure political participation, just as there is a North American bias in the belief that Mass attendance measures religious participation (see, for example, Thomas Bruneau, *The Church in Brazil: The Politics of Religion.* Austin: University of Texas Press, 1982, p. 31). The Brazilian context may require different criteria for measuring both political and religious participation.

[14]I was fortunate in that many of my contact persons in Brazil were pastoral agents who were very much trusted by members of basic ecclesial communities. Since that trust seemed to be extended to me, people spoke very freely about their social-political involvements. It should be noted that, in those few situations into which I entered without the help of pastoral agents, it took longer to win people's trust.

[15]Pedro A. Ribeiro de Oliveira, "Oprimidos: A Opcão Pela Igreja" (*Revista Eclesiástica Brasileira* 40, 158), pp. 643-653.

12
REFLECTIONS

I. Pastoral Documents

The Brazilian Catholic Church provides a clear illustration of how a new development in religious belief may in some sense be both a consequence of changes in the larger social context — such as industrialization, urbanization, the capitalization of agricultural production and the emergence of poor people's movements — and a stimulus to further social change, particularly in relation to human rights and economic justice. Furthermore, this situation also presents an interesting paradox, specifically that actions initially taken for religiously conservative reasons may produce consequences that are revolutionary for both the Church and the larger society. Those actions of the hierarchy that may have been motivated by institutional self-preservation — that is, defending the Faith against socialism, religious syncretism and Protestantism — eventually contributed to the development of a new ecclesial position — the preferential option for the poor — that is now leading to visible grassroots activism in both the religious and the political domains. Once this option became integrated into Catholic belief, with a theology rooting it in Scripture and in papal encyclicals, it could become somewhat independent of the vested interests of religious and secular elites. Thus, after the coup of 1964, the option for the poor would serve a relatively autonomous function in relation to the new military regime. The very Church position that had started as a means of protecting the faithful against a perceived Communist threat would later lead the bishops to speak out against the economic hardships and the repression occurring under the right-wing government.

Nevertheless, it must be asked how far the "official Church" (that is, the hierarchy) will go in promoting religious and social change, as well as exactly what kind of change it will promote. First of all, it must be recalled that the preferential option for the poor is a minority position, although it is the position of a very influential minority. Even the optimistic suggestion that this option represents the Church of the future[1] might imply that it is not fully representative of the Church of the present.

In terms of the future, there are no indications that the hierarchy will adopt a totally revolutionary position vis-à-vis society. In other words, the bishops are not about to advocate an armed uprising with the goal of establishing a socialist system. In particular, there are still strong denunciations of violent revolution.[2] In decribing the political positions of the most progressive bishops, one would have to call them "very liberal," in terms of a general position that seems to advocate the piecemeal reform of the existing social system. This is not to say, however, that people in other sectors within the Church — including some lay people, pastoral agents and theologians — do not hold more radical positions, such as the belief that, in order to eliminate poverty and injustice, there must be drastic restructuring of the present society.

With regard to relations of power within the Church itself, there are no indications that the bishops are about to relinquish their authority. The specifically pastoral activities of lay people, sisters and priests are still subject to the consent of the local bishops, and, furthermore, the pastoral activities of sisters and lay people are subject to the consent of the parish priest. When the local bishop happens to be progressive, the other members of the Church are allowed, and sometimes even encouraged, to take a great deal of initiative.

At the same time, it should not be inferred that the decisions of progressive bishops are made in a vacuum. Those bishops who are open to learning from the People of God sometimes become even more progressive as a result of input from people at the grassroots. So, although the fundamental structure of religious power has not changed, there has been occurring in many dioceses a dynamic process of mutual influence between the bishops and the lay people, particularly the lay people of the poorer classes. This dynamic process is both a consequence of and a source for further development in the preferential option for the poor.

In relation to power structures outside the Church, there is presently much discussion of the political consequences of the basic ecclesial communities. Some confusion may exist because of different interpretations of the word "political." As was mentioned earlier, observers who expected the CEBs to have an effect on party politics in the election of 1982 were very disappointed. However, in terms of other forms of political organizing — rural and urban labor unions, neighborhood associations, mobilization around local issues — experiences and understanding which people derive from their participation in CEBs seems to carry over into a certain type of social empowerment. It is in such areas that we should look for the "political" consequences of the basic ecclesial communities.

There are pastoral implications to be derived from the information that has been presented in this book. One is the importance of understanding the social context in which pastoral work is to be done. It seems clear that the Church in Brazil has benefitted from the use of social research to inform pastoral planning.

Another pastoral implication is the importance of listening to the lay people in order to integrate religious belief into a context that is meaningful to their lives. Those dioceses with the greatest vitality seem to be the ones in which the insights of lay people — particularly poor people — are solicited and utilized in pastoral planning. On the local level, people seem to respond particularly well to those pastoral agents who are able to communicate in terms relevant to the people's own reality.[3]

A third pastoral issue relates to the question of whether the contemporary Brazilian Catholic Church is really being "born of the people." An affirmative response to this question might be based more on wishful thinking than on social reality. One might suggest that those pastoral agents who persist in believing that all insights and decisions in the basic communities are coming from the poor people — hence denying their own input — may not be conscious of their own possible manipulation of the pedagogical process. In this light, these middle-class persons need to acknowledge and to work within their educative role, recognizing the importance of their particular contribution to the development of the social and ecclesial consciousness and consequently to the empowerment of oppressed people. Without conscientization, assisted by the pastoral agents, it seems likely that many people of the poorer classes would continue with the religious style that has always given them comfort in their sufferings — that is, miracle cults and millenarianism. With conscientization, however, people may develop a genuine hope of being able to change their situation.

It should be clear from this account of the development of the preferential option for the poor that religion is a semi-autonomous social element that interacts with other societal forces and that is not merely determined by them. At the same time, religion is not politically neutral. By conscious choice or by default, the actions of religious believers and religious leaders serve to provide support either for existing political-economic arrangements or for social change. Writings from the Hebrew prophets to modern papal encyclicals indicate that there is a potential within the Judeo-Christian tradition for generating opposition to dehumanizing social structures. It is a challenge for social scientists to discover the social-historical dynamics that prepare the way for that potential to be realized. There is further challenge of conscience for individual religious believers to discover the spiritual and concrete means by which God may prepare the way for that potential to be realized through our own human actions in the social world.

NOTES

[1]Penny Lernoux, "Brazil: The Church of Tomorrow" (*Lucha*, July-August, 1977), pp. 11-16.

[2]The 1983 *Campanha da Fraternidade* (Brotherhood Campaign) of the CNBB was centered on the slogan, "Brotherhood, yes! Violence, no!" I found it interesting that people in some of the CEBs which I visited interpreted this slogan not as a warning against violent revolution but rather as an indictment of the landowners and the military for their violence against peasants and workers.

[3]See Chapter Nine, Section IV.

APPENDIX I

RESEARCH METHODOLOGY

The preparation for the research on which this book was based began several years ago, when I became interested in the social roots of religious ideas, and, more specifically, of the theology of liberation. A search for the social-historical origins of that theology led me to focus attention on Latin America. In the process of two years of library research, it became increasingly clear that every significant sociological or religious factor that had contributed to the emergence of liberation theology, or to the more general phenomenon of the preferential option for the poor (of which the theology is the intellectual expression), seemed to have appeared first in Brazil.

About this time I began to make contact with people who had experience with the Brazilian Catholic Church. I wrote to Paulo Freire and subsequently interviewed him when he came to the United States. It was Professor Freire who persuaded me that a trip to Brazil would be feasible, offering help in finding housing, as well as introductions to some members of the hierarchy. With this encouragement, I began to make other contacts, through academic persons and missionaries, both in Brazil and in the United States, and, in this country, began interviewing persons who had worked within the Brazilian Catholic Church. During this time, I was also reading Brazilian religious and sociological journals collected at the Widener Library at Harvard University (which has the *Brazilian Ecclesiastical Review* as far back as 1960) in order both to familiarize myself with the relevant Brazilian literature and to trace the development of current Catholic belief. I continued writing to people in Brazil in the effort to establish further contacts and to make preliminary arrangements for field research.

I finally was able to go to Brazil from May to September of 1983, spending time in the states of Maranhão, Pernambuco,

Paraiba, Rio Grande do Norte, Rio de Janeiro, and Sao Paulo. The itinerary was determined by the occurrence of specific events (such as meetings of basic community representatives) and the presence of key informants at certain times and places. I spent the greatest amount of time (a little over three months) in the Northeast, particularly in the rural areas, because this was the location of some of the earliest changes in the Brazilian Catholic Church. The method which developed was about equally balanced between participant observation and interviewing, supplemented where possible by archival research.

I. Participant Observation

I spent the first month living in a rural village, in order to acquire some familiarity with the type of milieu in which many of the early religious innovations had developed. My first contact person was a North American Catholic missionary sister, who introduced me to the people in the village as the student of one of her colleagues in the United States who wanted to live with them for a few weeks in order to get to know their way of life. (At other times, people introduced me as a sociologist, a social worker, a student, and a friend from home. The most difficult situations were those in which I was not given any introduction at all, since these required additional time to gain people's trust. Fortunately that type of situation did not occur very often.) The introduction from a trusted pastoral agent was an instant means of entry, with a very warm and hospitable welcome, into this community.

In addition to visiting every household in the village and taking a census (a personal favor to my missionary friend and also a useful way of getting acquainted with the villagers), I took notes on all aspects of life there, particularly religious life. Becoming totally immersed in the way of life was both a choice and a necessity, since I saw no realistic alternatives. I slept in a hammock, bathed in a natural spring, washed my clothes in the same, ate a lot of rice and beans and *farinha* (manioc meal), got bitten by mosquitos, and tried to become accustomed to the absence of solitude in a community where it was apparently considered discourteous to leave a person alone. By choice, I also attempted to help with some common tasks, such as picking vegetables, feeding the chickens, shelling beans, and beating agricultural pests with home-made brooms.

This first phase was the most intensive period of participant observation. Later I visited and observed eight basic ecclesial communities (CEBs) — four rural and four urban — in five different states. Whenever possible, I tried to live with or near people in CEBs, which amounted to about half of the total time spent in Brazil. In addition to taking notes on interviews and observations, I also wrote notes on conversations with members of CEBs and with pastoral agents. The transcribed notes totalled two hundred fifteen single-spaced typewritten pages, ninty-one of which were taken in the course of participant observation.

During the five weeks in Pernambuco and two weeks in São Paulo, methods other than participant observation demanded more of my attention. However, I tried not to neglect opportunities for further observations and note-taking. Through a friend in Maranhão, I got in touch with a priest on the periphery of Recife, who gave me a warm welcome and invited me to visit any parish activities at any time. During my final week in Recife, I had the opportunity to live in this parish.

From Recife, I traveled to three other dioceses in neighboring states. In each place, I observed a meeting of a basic community, and in one diocese also observed a rural union meeting organized by a priest.

In São Paulo, the wealth of contacts was greatly out of proportion to the amount of time I was able to spend there. After my long stay in the Northeast, I had only two weeks left for

São Paulo, where I had made a wide variety of contacts through academic persons, missionaries, and other Church people, both in the United States and in other parts of Brazil. In addition to conducting interviews, I had the opportunity to visit two parishes on the periphery, staying overnight in one and for several days and nights in the other; to talk informally with several lay people and pastoral agents; to attend Sunday Mass, one basic community meeting, two youth meetings, and a large regional gathering at which lay representatives of CEBs met with their auxiliary bishop to present their input into pastoral planning.

In São Paulo I also had further experience of the great value of pastoral agents in providing instant entry into a community. Although my visits were brief, people seemed very open and friendly toward me when I was introduced by their parish priest. They allowed me to attend CEB meetings, and were very cooperative in granting interviews. In another situation, however, the introduction was less direct — an academic person asked a priest to get in touch with the daughter of a man whom I wished to interview. Although this man and his wife finally did grant me a tape-recorded interview, and were very helpful and hospitable, they were hesitant at first, and it was clear that they were not certain whether to trust me.

II. Interviews

The total number of formal interviews obtained was sixty-four — sixteen during preliminary research in the United States and forty-eight in Brazil. Approximately one-half were tape-recorded. Subjects included members of basic communities, middle-class lay people (three of whom were not affiliated with the Catholic Church, but rather with non-religious political movements), religious sisters, seminarians, priests, sociologists, theologians, bishops, and archbishops.

In Maranhão, I conducted only six interviews. In that state there were very few people who had information relevant to the topic on which I was focusing the interviews — that is, the historical reconstruction of the development of the preferential option for the poor. The situation was very different in Pernambuco, where I experienced a virtual explosion of very valuble contacts. I arrived there with the names and addresses of only three people. These persons put me in touch with others, setting up a chain reaction that resulted in twenty interviews in the city of Recife alone and five others in Paraíba and Rio Grande do Norte. Among all these people there were two in particular who were also helpful in periodically offering advice and orientation in the course of my research.

Contacts made during the week I spent in Rio de Janeiro were few but all valuable. With the help of people in other regions, I was able to get in touch with and interview the former national director of the Basic Education Movement, three former MEB staff members who had also been Catholic Action militants, and one of the key lay people who had helped to organize the Natal Movement. Rio was also the location of some very helpful sociological orientation, in the form of a discussion of my research with Father Clodovis Boff.

The two weeks in São Paulo were particularly intense. In addition to the participant observation described above, I interviewed twelve persons, including members of basic communities, former Catholic Actionists, theologians, sociologists, and the cardinal-archbishop, and also had some critical discussions of my work with academic persons.

The interviews were the most satisfying part of the research. I had not expected my contacts to be so productive, and was pleasantly surprised to find that (1) some of the people were even *in* Brazil (they had recently returned from exile), (2) that bishops and other well-known persons were so accessible, and

(3) that so many people were willing to talk so openly with a foreigner. Perhaps part of their willingness could be attributed to the nature of my contacts. In some instances I was introduced to people by priests or nuns. In addition, I had a letter of introduction from a North American nun and sociologist, who is known and respected among Church people in both the United States and Brazil. This letter was especially helpful in making contact with people in official and administrative positions.

III. Archival Research

I spent the least time on archival research, finding it much more interesting to learn from living people than from documents, particularly since the history I was reconstructing was so recent that most of the people who experienced it are still alive and clear of memory. In order to allow adequate time for interviews, I tried to locate written materials that could be either purchased or photocopied and studied after I returned to the United States. These included several documents of the National Conference of the Brazilian Bishops, including the pastoral plans of 1962 and 1965 (which were initially difficult to find, since they were out of print), as well as records of conferences of basic community representatives and some materials related to earlier social and religious movements.

IV. Reflections

In reflecting on the experience of my research in Brazil, two words that come to mind are exciting and disconcerting. An element of serendipity was present throughout much of the field work. There were some delightful and unexpected developments — particularly the opportunity to interview several persons whom I had not expected to meet. Another pleasant discovery was the warm hospitality of everyone from poor farmers to bishops, as well as middle-class families and pastoral agents.

Finally, there is also a certain element of adventure in learning to exist, on an everyday basis, in relation to a language and a culture different from one's own. Although this may sometimes be difficult and even frustrating, it is also stimulating.

The disconcerting element was the challenge to the assumptions which I had formed during the preliminary stage of library research. Most of the written material available was religious literature, which appeared to present religious and social change as spontaneously emerging from the grassroots, and which also appeared to present basic ecclesial communities as involved in this change by means of a smooth internal process of relating spirituality to social activism. I initially accepted these ideas. In the course of my field research, however, I discovered that the internal process in the CEBs was much more haphazard than what was presented in the literature, and that activism toward religious and social change was being facilitated by middle-class pastoral agents. The reasons for the discrepancies between the literature and the reality gradually became clear to me. First of all, religious writings often focus on an ideal toward which to strive, but to an outsider they may appear to be describing what already exists. Second, many of the writers have never been pastorally involved in an ongoing way with a basic community, but rather base their books and articles on observations of large semi-annual meetings of CEB representatives, which are more highly structured than the local weekly meetings. Third, the idea that change is arising from the poor people themselves is a meaningful part of the belief system of progressive Brazilian Catholics, but personal meaning does not always necessarily coincide with empirically observable sociological reality.

Since it is a task of social scientists to question the commonly accepted definitions of situations, I was rather embarrassed to discover that I had absorbed the very ideological position that was central to the phenomenon that I was studying. Fortunately, this discovery occurred before I had conducted many of the interviews, so that there was likely no more than the usual degree of observer bias that is characteristic of social research.

One final comment about bias — I belong to the school of sociology that advocates the acknowledgment, rather than the attempted elimination, of one's religious, ethical, and political positions. My personal values include a belief in the unity of religious and social concerns, leading me to be in sympathy with those Church people who are committed to the preferential option for the poor. However, it should be obvious from the preceding discussion that my research challenged the assumptions that were a consequence of that sympathy, and that I try to remain open to such challenges. Although it may not be humanly possible to be always completely free of bias, I have endeavored to render an accurate description of the facts as they have presented themselves.

APPENDIX II

LIST OF ABBREVIATIONS

ACO	*Acão Católica Operária* (Workers' Catholic Action)
ACR	*Acão Católica Rural* (Rural Catholic Action)
AP	*Acão Popular* (Popular Action)
CEB	*Comunidade Eclesial de Base* (Basic ecclesial community)
CEBRAP	*Centro Brasileiro de Análise e Planejamento* (Brazilian Center for Analysis and Planning)
CELAM	*Conferência Episcopal Latinoamericana* (Latin American Bishops' Conference)
CENFI	*Centro de Formação Intercultural* (Intercultural Formation Center)
CERIS	*Centro de Estatística Religiósa e Investigações Sociais* (Religious Statistics and Research Center)
CGT	*Comando Geral de Trabalhadores* (General Confederation of Workers)
CNBB	*Conferência Nacional dos Bispos do Brasil* (National Conference of Brazilian Bishops)
CPC	*Centro Popular de Cultura* (Popular Culture Center)
IBRADES	*Instituto Brasileiro de Desenvolvimento* (Brazilian Development Institute)
JAC	*Juventude Agrária Católica* (Young Catholic Farmers)
JEC	*Juventude Estudantil Católica* (Young Catholic Students)
JFC	*Juventude Feminina Católica* (Young Catholic Women)
JIC	*Juventude Independente Católica* (Independent Catholic Youth)
JMC	*Juventude Masculina Católica* (Young Catholic Men)
JOC	*Juventude Operária Católica* (Young Catholic Workers)
JUC	*Juventude Universitária Católica* (Young Catholic University Students)

LADOC	Latin American Documentation
LEC	*Liga Eleitoral Católica* (Catholic Electoral League)
MCP	*Movimento de Cultura Popular* (Popular Culture Movement)
MEB	*Movimento de Educação de Base* (Basic Education Movement)
MMM	*Movimento por um Mundo Melhor* (Movement for a Better World)
PE	*Plano de Emergência* (Emergency Plan)
Pe.	*Padre* (Father, as in the title of a priest)
PPC	*Plano de Pastoral de Conjunto* (Unified Pastoral Plan)
PT	*Partido de Trabalhadores* (Workers' Party)
PUC	*Pontifícia Universidade Catolica* (Pontifical Catholic University)
REB	*Revista Eclesiástica Brasileira (Brazilian Ecclesiastical Review)*
SAPPP	*Sociedade Agrícola e Pecuária dos Plantadores de Pernambuco* (Agricultural Society of Planters and Cattlemen of Pernambuco)
SAR	*Serviço de Assistência Rural* (Rural Assistance Service)
SORPE	*Serviço de Orientação Rural de Pernambuco* (Rural Orientation Service of Pernambuco)
SUDENE	*Superintendência de Desenvolvimento do Nordeste* (Superintendency of Development of the Northeast)
UNE	*União Nacional dos Estudantes* (National Student Union)

APPENDIX III

PERSONS MENTIONED OR QUOTED MORE THAN ONCE IN THE TEXT

Dom Paulo Evaristo Arns — Cardinal-Archbishop of São Paulo.

Miguel Arraes — Governor of Pernambuco at the time of the Coup of 1964; presently a national congressman.

Marina Bandeira — Former national director of the Basic Education Movement; presently with the regional Justice and Peace Office in Rio de Janeiro.

Clodovis Boff — Brazilian priest, theologian and sociologist.

Leonardo Boff — Brazilian priest, theologian and editor of the *Revista Eclesiástica Brasileiro (REB — Brazilian Ecclesiastical Review)*.

Dom Hélder Pessoa Câmara — Recently retired Archbishop of Olinda and Recife; formerly national Catholic Action chaplain, secretary general of the CNBB and auxiliary bishop of Rio de Janeira; helped reorganize Catholic Action in 1950; helped organize the CNBB in 1952, CELAM in 1955 and the Medellín conference (CELAM II) in 1968.

Dom Jaime Câmara — Cardinal-Archbishop of Rio in the 1950's and 1960's; president of the CNBB in the early 1960's.

General Humberto de Alencar Castelo Branco — one of the key leaders of the 1964 coup and the first of five military presidents.

Dom Marcelo Cavalheira — Bishop of Guarabira, PB; former rector of the regional seminary in Olinda; also a former Catholic Action chaplain.

Dom Sebastião Leme de Silveira Cintra — Cardinal-Archbishop of Rio during the *Estado Novo;* helped to re-establish strong Church-state relations.

Dom António Costa — presently auxiliary bishop of Natal.

Paulo Crespo — organizer of SORPE; presently coordinator for pastoral action in Northeast Region II.

Dom José Delgado — former archbishop of São Luis, who was known for his encouragement of pastoral innovations.

Dom Luis Fernandes — bishop of Campina Grande, PB; a former Catholic Action chaplain.

Dom António Fragoso — bishop of Crateús, CE; formerly auxiliary bishop of São Luis; former Catholic Action chaplain.

Paulo Freire — author of *Pedagogy of the Oppressed;* a pioneer in adult literacy and cultural education; presently Professor of Education at PUC/São Paulo.

João Goulart — President of Brazil from 1961 to 1964.

Francisco Julião — Organizer of numerous peasant leagues from 1955 to 1964; national deputy until 1964.

Juscelino Kubitschek — President of Brazil from 1956 to 1960.

Dom Aloíso Lorsheider — President of the CNBB.

Mons. Expedito Sobral de Medeiros —Pastor of São Paulo do Potengí; one of the organizers of the Natal Movement.

Dom Nivaldo Monte — Present Archbishop of Natal and one of the organizers of the Natal Movement.

Jánio Quadros — President of Brazil for brief period in 1961.

Dom Eugênio Sales — One of the early innovators in the Church in Northeast Brazil; organized the Natal Movement; presently Cardinal-Archbishop of Rio de Janeiro.

Lourdes Santos — A lay person and Catholic Actionist who helped organize the Natal Movement.

Dom José Lamartine Soares — Auxiliary Bishop of Olinda and Recife; former Catholic Action chaplain.

Dom José Vicente Távora — A former Catholic Action chaplain who was instrumental in organizing MEB.

Getúlio Vargas — Dictator from 1930 to 1945; president of Brazil from 1951 to 1954.

Francisco Whitaker — a lay person and former JUCist who was one of the writers of the Unified Pastoral Plan (PPC).

APPENDIX IV

TABLES

Table 1 — General Statistics for the Brazilian Catholic Church

YEAR	1965	1975	1981
Number of Dioceses and Prelacies	189	217	236
Number of Parishes	4,764	5,947	6,415
Number of Priests			
Secular	4,872	4,990	5,172
Religious	7,495	7,634	7,564
Total	12,376	12,624	12,736
Number of Religious (other than priests)			
Sisters	40,141	38,527	37,691
Brothers	1,932	1,541	1,395
Lay Brothers	1,811	1,185	1,082
Inhabitants per Diocese or Prelacy	458,094	483,559	515,030
Inhabitants per Parish	18,174	17,645	18,947
Inhabitants per Priest	7,001	8,312	9,544

SOURCES: Unified Pastoral Plan (1965)
　　　　　CERIS (1975 and 1981)

Table 2 — Native and Foreign Clergy (1970-1981)

YEAR	1970	1981	Percent Change
Secular Priests			
Brazilian	3,901	4,051	+3.84%
Foreign	1,103	1,096	−0.63%
(Undeclared)	(82)	(25)	
Total	5,086	5,172	+1.69%
Religious Priests			
Brazilian	3,794	3,773	−0.55%
Foreign	4,270	3,791	−11.21%
(Undeclared)	(2)	(0)	
Total	8,066	7,564	−6.22%
All Priests			
Brazilian	7,695	7,824	+1.67%
Foreign	5,373	4,887	−9.04%
(Undeclared)	(84)	(25)	
Total	13,152	12,736	−3.16%

SOURCE: CERIS

APPENDIX V

Glossary

accompany — to facilitate the spiritual formation and the conscientization of people in a basic ecclesial community.

assistentialism — almsgiving.

base —grassroots.

basic ecclesial community (CEB) — a unit smaller than a parish; a group of ten to thirty people who may gather together for prayer, mutual aid, Scriptural reflection and/or political action.

basic (grassroots) education — see conscientization.

Catholic Action — an institutionalized form of lay participation in the Church.
    General (Italian) Catholic Action — movement oriented toward traditional piety, controlled by local bishop, and divided by age and sex.
    Specialized (French/Belgian) Catholic Action — movement oriented toward lay leadership and lay spiritual formation, emphasizing youth groups divided according to social milieu.

capitalization — the transformation of the feudal relations of production to capitalist relations of production (e.g., peasants become wage workers; wealth is based not so much on land as on the capital to be invested in land, equipment, labor and the production of specific cash crops).

conscientization — the process of encouraging poor people to learn to perceive social, political, economic and cultural contradictions and to take action against oppressive structures.

corporatism — the organization of interest groups into vertical categories controlled by a strong central government.

engenho — a sugar plantation.

favela — a sqatter settlement on the periphery of a city.

grileiro — a land speculator who uses forged papers to remove farmers from public land to which they have the legal right (as squatters).

historical consciousness — the awareness of a subordinated class of their role in transforming the structure of their society.

human promotion — see *promoção humana.*

institutionalization — the establishment of a permanent pattern, such as the official approval by the Brazilian bishops of the preferential option for the poor.

interior — a rural area in Brazil.

liberation theology — the intellectual articulation of the belief that people's eternal salvation is inseparable from their involvement in the struggle toward the creation of a just society.

pastoral agents — lay people, sisters and priest who work with the poor, particularly those who work to facilitate the process of conscientization in basic ecclesial communities.

populism — the manipulation of the democratic sentiments of the masses by politicians who claim to represent their interests.

promoção humana (literally "human promotion") — the social, economic and cultural betterment of the poor as a goal of the work of religious activists.

prophetic — challenging both religious and political structures to meet the norms of justice expressed in religious teaching (as found in the Bible and in Papal Encyclicals).

sertão — the semi-arid countryside of northeast Brazil.

sindicato — labor, trade or rural union.

spiritism (or spiritualism) — a set of beliefs and practices based on the idea that the dead communicate with the living; sometimes combined with rituals of healing.

syncretism — the combing of symbols and beliefs from different religions — such as folk Catholicism, spiritualism and/or African and Native American cults.

zona da mata — the forest region of Pernambuco, located between the coastal area and the *sertão,* and characterized by the intensive production of sugar cane.

Bibliography

Alves, Marcio Moreira
1973   *A Grain of Mustard Seed.* Harmondsworth, England:
        Penguin Books.
1979   *A Igreja e a Política no Brasil.* São Paulo: Editora
        Brasiliense.

Alves, Rubem
1978   "A Volta do Sagrado: Os Caminhos da Sociologia da
        Religião no Brasil." *Religião e Sociedade* 3: 109-141.

Azevedo, Fernando António
1982   *As Ligas Camponesas.* Rio de Janeiro: Paz e Terra.

Azzi, Riolando
1978   *O Catolicismo Popular no Brasil: Aspectos Históricos.*
        Petrópolis: Vozes.

Barreiro, Alvaro
1982   *Basic Ecclesial Communities: The Evangelization of the
        Poor.* Maryknoll, N.Y.: Orbis Books.

Barros, Raimundo Caramuru de
1968   *Brasil: Uma Igreja em Renovação.* Petrópolis: Vozes.

Berryman, Philip
1981   "Latin America: 'Iglesia que nace del pueblo.' " *Christianity
        and Crisis* (September 21): 238-242.

Boff, Clodovis
1979   "A Influência Política das Comunidades Eclesiais de Base
        (CEBs)." *Religião e Sociedade* 4: 95-119.
1980a   *Agente Pastoral e Povo.* Petrópolis: Vozes.
1980b   "CEBs e Prática da Libertação." *Revista Eclesiástica
        Brasileira* 40, 160: 595-625.

Boff, Leonardo
1977   "A Igreja e a Paixão do Povo." *Religião e Sociedade* 1:
        115-118.
1978   *Jesus Christ Liberator: A Critical Christology for Our
        Time.* Maryknoll, N.Y.: Orbis Books.

Brazilian Bishops of the Center-West Region
1973 "A Marginalização de um Povo." Reprinted in Luiz
Gonzaga de Souza Lima, *Evolução Política dos Católicos e
da Igreja no Brasil.* Petrópolis: Vozes, pp. 200-239.

Brazilian Bishops and Religious Superiors
of the Northeast
1973 *Eu Ouvi os Clamores do Meu Povo.*
Salvador: Editora Beneditina.

Bruneau, Thomas
1974 *The Political Transformation of the Brazilian Catholic
Church.* London: Cambridge University Press.
1980 "Basic Christian Communities in Latin America: Their
Nature and Significance." In Daniel R. Levine (Ed.),
Churches and Politics in Latin America. Beverly Hills:
Sage Publications, pp. 225-237.
1982 *The Church in Brazil: The Politics of Religion.* Austin:
University of Texas Press.

Callado, António
1980 *Tempo de Arraes.* Rio de Janeiro: Paz e Terra.

Camargo, Cándido Procópio Ferreira de
1979 *Igreja e Desenvolvimento.* São Paulo: Editora Brasileira de
Ciências.

Camargo, Cándido Procópio Ferreira de, *et al.*
1982 *São Paulo 1975: Crescimento e Pobreza.* São Paulo: Edições
Loyola.

Cardijn, Joseph
1955 *Challenge to Action.* Chicago: Fides.

Cassidy, Sally Whelan
1959 *Some Aspects of Lay Leadership.* Unpublished doctoral
dissertation, University of Chicago.

Cavalheira, Dom Marcelo Pinto
1983 "Momentos Históricos e Desdobramentos de Ação Católica
Brasileira." *Revista Eclesiástica Brasileira* 43, 169: 10-28.

Coleman, William J.
1958 *Latin American Catholicism: A Self-Evaluation.*
Maryknoll, N.Y.: Maryknoll Publications.

Conferência Nacional dos Bispos do Brasil (CNBB)
    1962   Plano de Emergência. Rio de Janeiro: Livraria Dom Bosco
            Editora.
    1966   *Plano de Pastoral de Conjunto.* Rio de Janeiro: Livraria
            Dom Bosco Editora.
    1967a   "Nossas Responsibilidades em Face da 'Populorum
            Progressio' e das Conclusões de Mar del Plata." *Revista
            Eclesiástica Brasileira* 27, 2: 469-474.
    1967b   "Missão da Hierarquia no Brasil de Hoje." *Revista
            Eclesiástica Brasileira* 27, 4: 1088-1112.
    1977   *Comunicacão Pastoral ao Povo de Deus.* São Paulo: Edições
            Paulinas.
    1980   *Exigências Cristãs de Uma Ordem Política.* Porto Alegre:
            Edições Paulinas.

Comissão Pastoral da Terra
    1983   *CPT: Pastoral e Compromisso.* Petrópolis: Vozes.

Congar, Yves
    1965   *Lay People in the Church.* Westminster, Md.: Newman
Press.

Cussianovich, Alejandro
    1979   *Religious Life and the Poor.* Maryknoll, N.Y.: Orbis Books.

De Broucker, José
    1970   *Dom Helder Camara: The Violence of a Peacemaker.*
            Maryknoll, N.Y.: Orbis Books.

De Kadt, Emanuel
    1970   *Catholic Radicals in Brazil.* London: Oxford University
            Press.

Della Cava, Ralph
    1970   *Miracle at Joaseiro.* New York: Columbia University Press.

Didonet, Frederico
    1964   "Luzes e Sombras nos Movimentos Especializados."
            Revista Eclesiástica Brasileira 24, 3: 561-565.

Dodson, Michael
    1979   "The Catholic Left in Latin American Politics." *Journal of
            Interamerican Studies and World Affairs* 21, 1: 45-68.

Dussel, Enrique
    1976   *History and the Theology of Liberation.* Maryknoll, N.Y.:
            Orbis Books.

Erickson, Kenneth Paul
1977   *The Brazilian Corporative State and the Working-Class Politics.* Berkeley: University of California Press.

Evans, Peter
1979   *Dependent Development: The Alliance of Multinational, State, and Local Capital in Brazil.* Princeton, N.J.: Princeton University Press.

Ferrari, Alceu
1968   *Igreja e Desenvolvimento: O Movimento de Natal.* Natal: Federação José Augusto.

Fitzsimons, John, and Paul McGuire (Eds.)
1938   *Restoring All Things: A Guide to Catholic Action.* New York: Sheed and Ward.

Frank, André Gunder
1979   "On the Mechanics of Imperialism: The Case of Brazil." In K.T. Fann and Donald C. Hodges (Eds.), *Readings in U.S. Imperialism.* Boston: Porter Sargent.

Freire, Paulo
1970   *Pedagogy of the Oppressed.* New York: Seabury.
1974   "Conscientization." *Cross Currents 23, 1: 23-31.*

Gallet, Paul
1970   *Freedom to Starve.* Hammondsworth, England: Penguin Books.

Gutierrez, Gustavo
1973   *A Theology of Liberation.* Maryknoll, N.Y.: Orbis Books.

Hoornaert, Eduardo
1966   "A Igreja Diante de uma Nova Situação." *Revista Eclesiástica Brasileira* 26, 4: 872-884.
1967   "O Concílio Vaticano II e a Igreja no Brasil." *Revista Eclesiástica Brasileira* 27, 1: 43-45.

Horowitz, Irving L.
1964   *Revolution in Brazil.* New York: E. P. Dutton.

Houtart, François, and Emile Pin
1965   *The Church and the Latin American Revolution.* New York: Sheed and Ward.

Houtart, François, and André Rousseau
    1971   *The Church and Revolution.* Maryknoll, N.Y.: Orbis Books.

Humphrey, John
    1982   *Capitalist Control and Workers' Struggle in the Brazilian
            Auto Industry.* Princeton, N.J.: Princeton University Press.

Ianni, Octavio
    1970   *Crisis in Brazil.* New York: Columbia University Press.

Junqueira, José Cesar
    1975   "The Church in Brazil: A Stronghold of Opposition."
            Brazilian Studies 7:21-34.

Krischke, Paulo J.
    1977   "Nationalism and the Catholic Church: The Preparation
            for Democracy in Brazil." *LARU Studies* 1, 2: 62-93
            (Toronto: Latin American Research Unit).

Latin American Bishops' Conference (CELAM)
    1970   *The Church in the Present-Day Transformation of Latin
            America in the Light of the Council* (Medellín Documents).
            Bogotá: General Secretariat of CELAM.

Latin American Documentation (LADOC)
    1978   *Repression Against the Church in Brazil: 1968-1978.*
            LADOC Keyhole Series, No. 18. Washington, D.C.: United
            States Catholic Conference.

Leers, Bernardino
    1966   "Igreja e Desenvolvimento Rural." *Revista Eclesiástica
            Brasileira* 26, 2: 331-342.

Lernoux, Penny
    1977   "Brazil: The Church of Tomorrow." *Lucha* (July-August,
            1977): 11-16.
    1980   *The Cry of the People.* Garden City, N.Y.: Doubleday.

Lesbaupin, Ivo
    1980   "A Igreja Católica e os Movimentos Populares Urbanos."
            Religião e Sociedade 5: 189-198.

Libânio, João B.
    1979   "Igreja, Povo que se Liberta: III Encontro Inter-eclesial de
            Comunidades de Base." *Síntese* 5, 14: 93-110.

Libânio-Cristo, Carlos Alberto (Frei Beto)
1981   *O Que e Comunidade Eclesial de Base?* São Paulo: Brasiliense.

Lima, Luiz Gonzaga de Souza
1979   *Evolucão Política dos Católicos e da Igreja no Brasil.* Petrópolis: Vozes.

Maduro, Otto
1975   "Marxist Analysis and the Sociology of Religion." *Social Compass* 22, 3-4: 305-322.
1977   "New Marxist Approaches to the Relative Autonomy of Religion." *Sociological Analysis* 38: 359-367.
1979   *Religion y lucha de clases.* Caracas: Editorial Ateneo (English translation by Orbis Books, 1982).
1984   "Is Religion Revolutionary?" *New England Sociologist* 5, 1: 127-131.

Mainwariñg, Scott
1983   "The Catholic Youth Workers Movement (JOC) and the Emergence of the Popular Church in Brazil." Notre Dame, IN.: The Helen Kellogg Institute for International Studies, University of Notre Dame.

Malloy, James M.
1977   *Authoritarianism and Corporatism in Latin America.* Pittsburgh: University of Pittsburgh Press.

Margerie, Bertrand de
1963   "Pode o Católico de 1963 Dizer-Se Neo-Capitalista, Revolucionário ou Socialista?" *Revista Eclesiástica Brasileira* 23, 3: 687-700.

Marins, José
1976   "Basic Christian Communities in Latin America." *Basic Christian Communities* LADOC Keyhole Series Number 14. Washington, D.C.: U.S. Catholic Conference.

Martins, Carlos Estevam
1983   "História do CPC" (Photocopied article, source unknown).

Martins, Heloisa Helena T. de Souza
1980   "Igreja e Movimentos Populares Urbanos." *Religião e Sociedade* 5: 205-210.

Mecham, J. Lloyd
    1966   *Church and State in Latin America.* Chapel Hill, N.C.:
           University of North Carolina Press.

Medina, C.A. de, and Pedro A. Ribeiro de Oliveira
    1973   "A Igreja Católica no Brasil: Uma Perspectiva Sociologica."
           Revista Eclesiástica Brasileira 23, 129: 72-91.

Miguez Bonino, José
    1976   *Doing Theology in a Revolutionary Situation.* Philadelphia:
           Fortress Books.

Miranda José Porfirio
    1974   *Marx and the Bible: A Critique of the Philosophy of
           Oppression.* Maryknoll, N.Y.: Orbis Books.

Movimento de Cultura Popular (MCP)
    1963   "O Que é o MCP?" (Photocopied article, source unknown).

Mutchler, David E.
    1965   "Roman Catholicism in Brazil." *Studies in Comparative
           International Development* 1, 8: 103-117.

Neal, Marie Augusta
    1972   "How Prophecy Lives." *Sociological Analysis* 33, 3: 125-141.

Oliveira, Pedro A. Ribeiro de
    1977   "Presença da Igreja Católica na Sociedade Brasileira."
           Religião e Sociedade 1: 111-113.
    1979   "The 'Romanization' of Catholicism and Agrarian
           Capitalism in Brazil." *Social Compass* 26: 2-3.
    1980   "Opção pelos Pobres: Critérios Práticos." *Revista
           Eclesiástica Brasileira* 40: 158: 211-215.
    1981a "Oprimidos: A Opção Pela Igreja." *Revista Eclesiástica
           Brasileira* 41, 164: 643-653.
    1981b "Realizar Igreja Hoje: As CEBs." *Revista Eclesiástica
           Brasileira* 41, 164: 654-659.

Padin, Dom Candido
    1979   "A Doutrina da Seguranca Nacional à Luz da Doutrina
           Social da Igreja" (Reprinted in Lima, 1979: 150-167).

Palácio, Carlos
    1979   "Uma Consciência Histórica Irreversível." *Síntese* 6, 17:
           19-40.

Peruvian Bishops' Commission for Social Action
1969   *Between Honesty and Hope.* Maryknoll, N.Y.: Maryknoll
        Publications.

Pitt, James
1980   "The Process of Pastoral Planning." LADOC 10, 5: 1-11.

Quartim, José
1971   *Dictatorship and Armed Struggle in Brazil.* London: NLB.

Queiroga, Gervásio Fernandes de
1977   *CNBB: Comunhão e Corresponsabilidade.* São Paulo:
        Paulinas.

Roett, Riordan
1972   *Brazil in the Sixties.* Nashville: Vanderbilt University
        Press.

Salem, Helena, *et. al.*
1981   *A Igreja dos Oprimidos.* São Paulo: Brasil Debates.

Sanders, Thomas G.
1967   "Brazil's Catholic Left." *America* 117:
        598-601 in Brazil's Political Transition."
        Hanover, N.H.: American Universities Field Staff Reports.

Santos, Theotónio dos
1971   "The Structure of Dependency." In K.T. Fann and Donald
        C. Hodges (Eds.), *Readings in U.S. Imperialism.* Boston:
        Porter Sargent.

Schmitter, Philippe C.
1973   "The 'Portugalization' of Brazil," in Alfred Stepan (Ed.),
        Authoritarian Brazil: *Origins, Policies, and Future.* New
        Haven: Yale University Press, pp. 179-232.

Schneider, Ronald M.
1971   *The Political System of Brazil.* New York: Columbia
        University Press.

Skidmore, Thomas E.
1967   *Politics in Brazil, 1930-1964: An Experiment in Democracy.*
        New York: Oxford University Press.

Souza, Itamar de
1982   *A Luta da Igreja Contra os Coroneis.* Petrópolis: Vozes.

Souza, Luiz Alberto Gomez de
1968   "Igreja e Sociedade: Elementos Para um Marco Teorico."
        Sintese 5, 13: 15-29.
1981   "Structures and Mechanisms of Domination." In Sergio
        Torres and John Eagleson (Eds.), *The Challenge of Basic
        Christian Communities*. Maryknoll, N.Y.: Orbis Books.
1982   *Clases Populares e Igreja nos Caminhos da História*.
        Petrópolis: Vozes.

Stein, Stanley J., and Barbara J. Stein
1970   *The Colonial Heritage of Latin America*. New York: Oxford
        University Press.

Stepan, Alfred (Ed.)
1973   *Authoritarian Brazil: Origins, Policies, and Future*. New
        Haven: Yale University Press.

Texeira, Faustino Luiz Couto
1982   *Comunidade Eclesial de Base: Elementos Explicativos de
        sua Génese*. Unpublished Master's Thesis, Department of
        Theology, Pontifícia Universidade Católica do Rio de
        Janeiro.

Torres, Sergio, and John Eagleson (Eds.)
1981   *The Challenge of Basic Christian Communities* (Papers
        from the International Ecumenical Congress of Theology,
        February 20—March 2, 1980, São Paulo). Maryknoll, N.Y.:
        Orbis Books.

Vallier, Ivan
1970   *Catholicism, Social Control, and Modernization in Latin
        America*. Englewood Cliffs, N.J.: Prentice-Hall. 1970.

Wanderley, Luiz Eduardo
1978   "Igreja e Sociedade no Brasil: 1950-64/1964-75." *Religião
        e Sociedade* 3: 93-107.
1982   *Educar Para Transformar: Educação Popular — Igreja
        Católica — Política no Movimento de Educacao de Base
        (MEB) — 1961-1965*. Unpublished Doctoral Dissertation
        in Sociology, Department of Social Sciences, Universidade
        de São Paulo.

Weffort, Francisco C.
1977   "E Por Que Não a Igreja na Política?" *Religião e Sociedade*
        1: 119-121.